DYNAMIC TR

Building Web Applications with React, Next.js & Tailwind

By Grace Huang

To my parents, who gave me my first computer in 1999.

Table of Contents

INTRODUCTION

I have a long history with web development. In 1999, when I was in high school, my parents gave me my first computer. I started tinkering with Microsoft FrontPage and built my early websites: fan websites for my favorite soccer players. To this day, I still think FrontPage was a powerful tool that made many amateurs like me get into Web 1.0.

What fascinated me about web development was how a few lines of HTML code in a plain text editor could turn into a web page. In 2006, I landed my first job as a web developer in New York City. At that time, jQuery was the prevalent utility in the industry. Despite the co-existence of many fragmented browsers, jQuery unified the DOM standards and brought backward compatibility.

In 2008, while working at a startup, I co-wrote a JavaScript Framework from scratch with a group of hardcore front-end engineers. It was pretty cool! Even though some people disliked JavaScript for its lack of types and believed it would be short-lived, I loved how flexible and ubiquitous this language was.

To this day, JavaScript is still not dead yet, but even more popular.

When I was running my business Roxy in 2016, React and Bootstrap were my primary go-to for building websites. React finally united HTML and JavaScript, and Bootstrap standardized the styles of UI components on both web and mobile.

Fast forward to 2023, React, Next.js, and Tailwind are now the go-to frameworks for building web applications. Almost every day, new applications pop up around the world using this trio. These frameworks have become stepping stones for engineers and entrepreneurs to launch their products at a speed that I could never have imagined 20 years ago.

This is why I wrote this book: to demonstrate how you can effectively utilize these three tools to build web applications, regardless of whether you are a software engineer helping adopt new web stacks or an entrepreneur starting a software business.

End Goal

After reading the book, you should be able to create web applications on your own and deploy them to the server, with the three tools: React, Next.js, and Tailwind CSS, and have the applications running under your domains

Web development will no longer be a mystery to you, and you will be familiar with the end-to-end process.

Structure

Over the years, I have found that the most effective way to teach others is through examples. Good examples are like good stories - they become the vehicle for showcasing the knowledge and skills you are acquiring. You may forget how a new concept was described, but you will always remember how you put it into practice.

With this same spirit, this book will focus more on doing, through real-time projects.

Part 1

The first part of this book will focus on getting you familiar with the Dynamic Trio of React, Next.js, and Tailwind, and what makes each of them individually powerful.

The chapters in this part will cover:

• Chapter 1: Introduction to React

• Chapter 2: Introduction to Next.js

• Chapter 3: Introduction to Tailwind CSS

However, we will not dive into the details of how to use them just yet. That will be covered in Part 2.

If you are already familiar with any of the concepts, feel free to skip this part.

Part 2

The second part of this book will be a step-by-step walkthrough of real-life web projects, guiding you through the process of creating these applications from scratch using the Dynamic Trio of React, Next.js, and Tailwind.

The chapters in this part will cover:

• Chapter 4: Building "Hello World"

• Chapter 5: Building A Personal Website

• Chapter 6: Building A Weather App

Part 3

The third part of this book will cover the necessary steps for deploying your application to production.

The chapter in this part will cover:

• Chapter 7: Deploying to Production

Prerequisites

To follow along with this book, you will need the following:

• Internet access

• A computer running either MacOS or Windows

• A Unix-specific Command Line Interface (CLI), a.k.a. Command Prompt, such as Terminal on Mac or Git Bash on Windows

- A text editor, such as VS Code or Sublime

- Node.js installed (version 14.6.0 or later)

Assumptions

This book assumes that you are new to web development with React, Next.js, and Tailwind, but not necessarily new to programming in general. If you have prior programming experience in other languages and knowledge of HTML, it should be easier to follow the steps in the book.

In addition, in this book, we will not cover setting up databases or scaling services, which are sizable topics themselves. We will focus on building user interfaces.

Finally, note that this book utilizes React version 18, Next.js version 13, and Tailwind version 3. Using different versions of these frameworks may result in variations.

Formats of the Book

As you follow along with the projects in the book, use these visual signals as a guide:

▷   : this means a step. You can follow it throughout the book for the actionable steps, and skim through other parts to save time.

>_   : this means a command line.

Let me explain: this means a deeper explanation for something being used in code or description.

Italic text often corresponds to keywords in the figures and code.

The code highlighted in gray refers to the area of focus or change, particularly for the file annotated with *(Partial)*, where only the changed code is shown due to the file size being too large to display in its entirety.

All the screenshots in this book are captured from a Mac computer.

In this book, the term *"Command Prompt"* refers specifically to the Command Line Interface (CLI) commonly used in Unix-based operating systems. On Mac, it is referred to as "Terminal", while on Windows, it may refer to "Git Bash" or "Cygwin", which are popular CLI alternatives for Windows users.

Code Examples

You can access all the code examples from this book for free at https:// github.com/higracehuang.

If you ever get lost in the book, the code examples will always be the best resource to get back on track. A direct link to the project repository will be provided at the end of each chapter in Part 2.

Getting Book Updates

I will do my best to keep the book up to date with the latest versions of React, Next.js, and Tailwind CSS.

To receive the latest updates on the book, subscribe to my mailing list by sending an email to higracehuang+dynamic-trio@gmail.com.

Suggestions

Please don't hesitate to provide feedback if anything is unclear or if you spot any typos in this book.

You can contact me through any of the following methods:

Email: higracehuang@gmail.com

Twitter: https://twitter.com/imgracehuang

LinkedIn: https://www.linkedin.com/in/lghuang/

Ready? Let's dive right in!

CHAPTER 1: INTRODUCTION TO REACT

What is React?

React is a JavaScript library for building user interfaces based on UI components, specifically designed for web applications.

It is named for its ability to react to changes in data and render the user interface accordingly. It reacts to changes in state and props and updates the UI to reflect those changes.

Let me explain: History of React

In 2011, Jordan Walke, a software engineer at Facebook, created React to address the challenge of managing constant updates and changes to the News Feed feature. The existing approach, which involved directly manipulating the DOM, was inefficient at handling frequent updates. To build a more efficient approach, Walke experimented with a new way of building UI, resulting in the creation of React.

React uses a virtual DOM to track changes to the user interface. When data changes, React updates the virtual DOM and compares it to the previous version. It then calculates the minimum number of changes required to bring the real DOM up to date with the virtual DOM. This approach makes React efficient and fast, even with large and complex user interfaces.

In this chapter, we will cover the basics of React, including components, JSX, props, and state, as well as the concept of virtual DOM.

Understanding the Virtual DOM

The React JavaScript library uses a programming concept called the *Virtual DOM*.

Problem with the Actual DOM

When a user interacts with a web page, the browser updates the DOM (Document Object Model) to reflect those changes.

However, updating the DOM can be a slow and expensive operation, especially for large and complex web pages. This is because the DOM is represented as a tree data structure, and after a change is made, the updated element and its children must be re-rendered to update the application's user interface (UI). This re-rendering, or re-painting, of the UI, can be slow and contribute to performance issues.

How the Virtual DOM Solves the Problem

To avoid these performance issues, React uses a Virtual DOM. **The Virtual DOM is an in-memory representation of the actual DOM.** It is a lightweight JavaScript object that contains all the necessary properties and attributes of the elements on a web page. When a change occurs in the user interface, React updates the Virtual DOM first, which is much faster than updating the actual DOM. Then, React compares the previous and updated Virtual DOMs and determines the minimum set of changes required to update the actual DOM. Finally, React applies those changes in a batch update to the actual DOM.

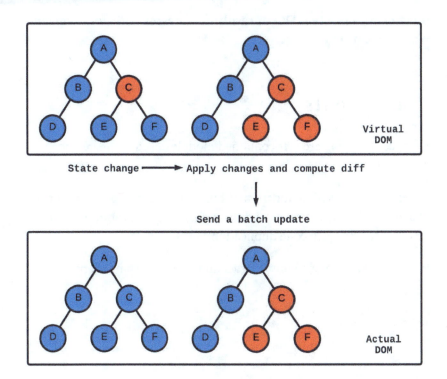

Figure 1-1 How React uses Virtual DOM to update UI

In Figure 1-1, the red circles represent the UI elements that have had their state changed. *Node C*, in particular, has changed, and because it has two leaf nodes (*Node E* and *Node F*), both nodes must be redrawn as well.

React uses a Virtual DOM to update the UI efficiently. Instead of triggering changes to the actual DOM, React creates a DOM structure in memory, applies the changes in the Virtual DOM, and computes the difference between the previous version of the Virtual DOM tree and the current Virtual DOM tree. Once the differences are identified (*Node C*, *Node E*, and *Node F*), React applies the minimal set of changes necessary to update the actual DOM to reflect the new state of the component.

Without the Virtual DOM, updating the DOM can be slow and inefficient, especially when dealing with large, complex UIs or frequent updates. **By using the Virtual DOM, React minimizes the number of** updates to the actual DOM, resulting in faster and more efficient web applications.

Components

React components are self-contained modules used to create user interfaces.

Like LEGO pieces, they function as building blocks, representing parts of a larger UI that can be reused throughout an application to improve efficiency and reduce code duplication.

Here's an example of a simple React app that uses components:

```
import React from 'react';

// Header component
function Header() {
  return (
    <header>
      <h1>My React App</h1>
    </header>
  );
}

// Main component
function Main() {
  return (
    <main>
      <h2>Welcome to my React App!</h2>
      <p>This is the main content area.</p>
    </main>
  );
}

// Footer component
function Footer() {
  return (
    <footer>
      <p>&copy; 2023 My React App</p>
    </footer>
  );
}

// App component that uses the Header, Main, and Footer components
function App() {
  return (
    <div>
      <Header />
      <Main />
      <Footer />
    </div>
  );
}
```

```
export default App;
```

In this example, we have three components: *Header*, *Main*, and *Footer*. Each component is a building block that can be combined to create a more complex application. The *App* component uses these three components to create a simple layout with a header, main content area, and footer.

JSX

JSX is React's syntax for creating components. It looks like HTML, but instead of just describing the structure of a webpage, you can also include JavaScript code to make your components dynamic and interactive.

Here is an example that demonstrates how JSX can be used to create dynamic and interactive web pages:

```
import React, { useState } from 'react';

function Counter() {
  const [count, setCount] = useState(0);

  function handleClick() {
    setCount(count + 1);
  }

  return (
    <div>
      <h1>Count: {count}</h1>
      <button onClick={handleClick}>Increment</button>
    </div>
  );
}

export default Counter;
```

In this example, we create a *Counter* component in React using JSX.

The component stores the current count in a state variable named *count* and updates the count using a function called *handleClick* when the user clicks the *Increment* button. Although the JSX code resembles HTML, we've included JavaScript code within curly braces {} to add interactivity to the component. Specifically, we use the *count* and *handleClick* variables to display the current count and handle user input.

By using JSX, we can create highly interactive components that respond to user input in real-time. This makes it easy to build dynamic web applications that provide an excellent user experience.

Later in the book, you will notice we use TSX instead of JSX. They are very similar. TSX, which stands for TypeScript JSX, is a variant of JSX that is specifically designed for use with TypeScript, a statically-typed superset of JavaScript. TypeScript provides additional features such as static typing, interfaces, and other advanced programming concepts, which can help improve code quality, maintainability, and developer productivity.

Props

In React, "*props*" is short for "*properties*" and is used to pass data from a parent component to a child component.

For example, a parent component could pass the string "Hello, world!" as a prop to a child component that displays that text.

Props can be any type of data, including strings, numbers, booleans, objects, and functions.

For example, consider the following component:

```
function Greeting(props) {
  return <h1>Hello, {props.name}!</h1>;
}
```

Here, the *Greeting* component takes a *props* parameter, which is an object containing the *name* property. The *name* property is used to render a greeting message.

When the component is used, it can be passed a *name* prop like so:

```
<Greeting name="John" />
```

In this example, the name *prop* is passed to the *Greeting* component with a value of "*John*". The component then renders the message "*Hello, John!*" using the *name* prop.

State

In React, a state is an object that contains data that determines the behavior and rendering of a component.

For example, a component that displays a counter might have a state object with a *count* property that keeps track of the current count.

When the state changes, React will automatically re-render the component with the new state, updating the user interface as necessary. This makes it easy to create dynamic and interactive UIs that respond to user input and other events.

You can define the state in a component using the *useState* hook. For example:

```
import React, { useState } from 'react';

function Example() {
  const [name, setName] = useState('');
  const [age, setAge] = useState(0);
  const [email, setEmail] = useState('');

  const handleNameChange = (e) => {
    setName(e.target.value);
  };

  const handleAgeChange = (e) => {
    setAge(e.target.value);
  };

  const handleEmailChange = (e) => {
    setEmail(e.target.value);
  };

  return (
    <div>
      <input type="text" placeholder="Name" value={name}
onChange={handleNameChange} />
      <input type="number" placeholder="Age" value={age}
onChange={handleAgeChange} />
      <input type="email" placeholder="Email" value={email}
onChange={handleEmailChange} />
      <p>{name} is {age} years old and their email is {email}.</p>
    </div>
  );
}

export default Example;
```

The *Example* component manages three states: *name*, *age*, and *email*. Each state is initialized using the *useState* hook, and its value can be updated using the corresponding setter function (*setName*, *setAge*, and *setEmail*).

The *handleNameChange, handleAgeChange,* and *handleEmailChange* functions are event handlers that update the state value when the input value changes.

Finally, the component renders the input fields and displays the current state values.

Conclusion

React is a powerful tool for building dynamic and responsive user interfaces. Its core concepts, including Virtual DOM, Components, JSX, Props, and State, have transformed front-end development and made it easier to create scalable and reusable UI components.

While this chapter does not provide any coding examples for you to play with, don't worry, we will provide projects in future chapters that allow you to apply the concepts you've learned about React.

React also has its limitations when it comes to building full-stack web applications, such as server-side rendering and routing. That's where Next.js comes in, providing a framework that simplifies these aspects of web development and addresses many of React's limitations.

Now, let's dive deeper into the features and benefits of Next.js.

CHAPTER 2: INTRODUCTION TO NEXT.JS

What is Next.js?

Next.js is an open-source web development framework built on top of React, which enables web applications with server-side rendering and generating static websites.

Let me talk about: History of Next.js[1]

Next.js was released by Vercel (formerly known as Zeit) in 2016. The framework was developed to address issues with React, which was popular at the time but had problems with accessibility, security, slow page loading times, and SEO. Next.js aimed to solve these issues, and has since gained popularity.

In 2019, Google began contributing to the project. Today, many large websites such as Walmart, Apple, Nike, Netflix, TikTok, Uber, Lyft, and Starbucks use the framework.

Next.js is often credited with completing React by offering the following features:

• Server-Side Rendering

• Static Site Generation

• Image Optimization

• Built-in Routing

These features have made Next.js a popular choice among developers looking to build powerful and performant web applications.

---

[1] History of Next.js: https://en.wikipedia.org/wiki/Next.js

Server-Side Rendering

One of the main advantages of Next.js is its ability to handle server-side rendering out of the box, which perfectly supplements React.

This means that your application can be rendered on the server before being sent to the client, which can result in faster initial page load times and better search engine optimization (SEO).

Server-Side Rendering with React Components

Let's say we have a simple React component called "*HomePage*" that we want to render on the server using Next.js.

Here's what the component might look like:

components/HomePage.jsx

```jsx
import React from 'react';

const HomePage = () => {
  return (
    <div>
      <h1>Welcome to my website!</h1>
      <p>This is the homepage.</p>
    </div>
  );
};

export default HomePage;
```

To render this component on the server using Next.js, we need to create a file called *pages/index.js*. This file will be automatically detected by Next.js and used as the homepage of our application.

Here's what *pages/index.js* might look like:

pages/index.js

```js
import HomePage from '../components/HomePage';

const IndexPage = () => {
  return <HomePage />;
};

export default IndexPage;
```

When a user visits our website, Next.js will first render this component on the server and return the HTML to the client. This means that the user will see the content of the page immediately, without having to wait for any JavaScript to load. Once the JavaScript loads, Next.js will then "hydrate" the page and turn it into a fully interactive React application.

This approach provides several benefits, including faster initial page load times, better search engine optimization, and improved accessibility.

Automatic Code Splitting

Next.js offers automatic code splitting, optimizing page load times by loading only the necessary code for each page.

Suppose we have a website with two pages: *HomePage* and *ContactPage*, each having its corresponding React component.

In a traditional React application, all the JavaScript code for both components would be bundled together into a single file that would be loaded when the user visits either page. This can result in slower page load times, particularly if the JavaScript code is large and complex.

However, with Next.js, each page is treated as a separate entry point for the application. Therefore, Next.js generates a separate JavaScript bundle for each page, containing only the necessary code for that specific page.

Here's what the *pages* folder might look like in a Next.js application:

```
/pages
    /index.js       // HomePage component
    /contact.js     // ContactPage component
```

When a user visits the *HomePage*, Next.js will load the JavaScript bundle for that page, which will contain only the necessary code for the *HomePage* component.

Similarly, when a user visits the *ContactPage*, Next.js will load the JavaScript bundle for that page, which will contain only the necessary code for the *ContactPage* component.

This approach reduces the amount of JavaScript required to load each page, optimizing page load times. It can also improve application performance by enabling better code size and complexity management.

Static Site Generation

Static site generation (SSG) is a powerful Next.js feature that generates a static HTML version of your website **at build time**. This can help to improve page load times, reduce server load, improve search engine optimization (SEO), and improve the user experience for your visitors.

With Next.js, you can use SSG to generate a fully functional website with dynamic data, without having to rely on server-side rendering or client-side JavaScript. This can be especially useful for websites with a large amount of content or for websites that don't require real-time updates.

To use SSG in Next.js, you can create a static page for each dynamic route using the *getStaticProps* function. This function allows you to fetch data from an external source and pass it as props to your component. You can then use this data to render the HTML for your page.

For example,

```
function Blog({ posts }) {
  return (
    <div>
      <h1>My Blog</h1>
      {posts.map(post => (
        <div key={post.id}>
          <h2>{post.title}</h2>
          <p>{post.body}</p>
        </div>
      ))}
    </div>
  );
}

export async function getStaticProps() {
  const res = await fetch('https://jsonplaceholder.typicode.com/posts');
  const posts = await res.json();

  return {
    props: {
      posts,
    },
  };
}
```

```
export default Blog;
```

In this example, we have a simple blog component that fetches data from the *jsonplaceholder* API using the *fetch* function. We then pass this data as props to the *Blog* component, which renders the HTML for each post.

The *getStaticProps* function is called at build time and fetches the data from the external API. This data is then passed as props to the *Blog* component, which is then rendered as a static HTML file.

Image Optimization

Next.js provides a range of built-in features that help to optimize images and improve the performance of your website.

Here are some of the key features related to image optimization:

Automatic Image Optimization

Next.js automatically optimizes images for you by providing multiple image sizes for different screen sizes, serving images in the optimal format, and providing lazy loading for images.

This helps to reduce the amount of data that needs to be downloaded by the user, resulting in faster page load times.

Automatic Format Selection

Next.js automatically serves images in the optimal format depending on the user's browser and device.

For example, if the user is using a browser that supports the WebP image format, Next.js will automatically serve WebP images instead of JPEG or PNG images.

This can help to further reduce the amount of data that needs to be downloaded, resulting in even faster page load times.

Lazy-Loading Images

Next.js supports lazy-loading of images, which means that images are only loaded when they are needed. This can help to reduce the initial page load time and improve the performance of your website.

Image Component

Next.js provides an *Image* component that makes it easy to include images on your website. This component supports automatic image optimization, lazy-loading, and multiple image sizes. Here's an example of how to use the *Image* component in Next.js:

```
import Image from 'next/image';

function MyComponent() {
  return (
    <div>
      <h1>My Component</h1>
      <Image
        src="/my-image.jpg"
        alt="My Image"
        width={500}
        height={500}
      />
    </div>
  );
}

export default MyComponent;
```

In this example, we have a simple component that includes an image using the *Image* component. We provide the image source, alt text, width, and height as props to the *Image* component. Next.js automatically optimizes the image and provides multiple sizes for different screen sizes.

Image optimization is an important aspect of website performance, and Next.js provides a range of built-in features that make it easy to optimize images and improve the performance of your website. By taking advantage of these features, you can ensure that your website loads quickly and provides a smooth and responsive user experience.

Built-in Routing

Next.js provides built-in routing that makes it easy to create dynamic and complex websites with multiple pages.

Here are some of the key features of Next.js routing.

File-based Routing

Next.js uses a file-based routing system, which means that each page in your website corresponds to a file in the *pages* directory.

Let's say you have a website with the following pages:

- *Home*

- *About*

- *Services*

- *Contact*

To create these pages in Next.js, you would create the following files in the *pages* directory:

```
pages/
├── index.js
├── about.js
├── services.js
└── contact.js
```

The *index.js* file corresponds to the homepage of your website, and the other files correspond to the other pages. For example, the *about.js* file would contain the code for the *About* page, the *services.js* file would contain the code for the *Services* page, and so on.

Here's an example of what the *about.js* file might look like:

pages/about.js

```
function AboutPage() {
  return (
    <div>
      <h1>About Us</h1>
      <p>We are a company that specializes in creating high-quality
websites.</p>
```

```
    </div>
  );
}

export default AboutPage;
```

In this example, we've created a simple *About* page component that contains a heading and some text. When a user visits the */about* route on our website, Next.js will automatically render this component and serve it as an HTML response to the user's browser.

Dynamic Routes

Next.js also supports dynamic routes, which allow you to create pages that can accept parameters in the URL.

Let's say you have a blog website where each blog post has a unique identifier (or "*slug*"). You want to create a dynamic route that can accept different slugs in the URL and display the corresponding blog post.

To create this dynamic route in Next.js, you would create a file called *[slug].js* in the *pages* directory. The square brackets [] around the file name indicate that this is a dynamic route that can accept parameters in the URL.

```
pages/
├── index.js
└── blog
    ├── [slug].js
```

Here's an example of what the *[slug].js* file might look like:

pages/blog/[slug].js

```
import { useRouter } from 'next/router';

function BlogPost() {
  const router = useRouter();
  const { slug } = router.query;

  return (
    <div>
      <h1>Blog Post: {slug}</h1>
      <p>This is the blog post with the slug {slug}.</p>
    </div>
  );
}

export default BlogPost;
```

In this example, we're using the *useRouter* hook from Next.js to get the current URL and extract the *slug* parameter from it. We then use this *slug* parameter to display the corresponding blog post.

For example, if a user visits the URL */blog/my-first-post*, Next.js will automatically route them to the *[slug].js* page and set the *slug* parameter to *my-first-post*. The *BlogPost* component will then be rendered with the correct *slug* parameter and display the corresponding blog post.

Nested Routes

Next.js also supports nested routes, which allow you to create pages with sub-paths.

For example, you could create a page for a blog post with the URL */blog/[slug]/comments*, where *[slug]* represents the unique identifier for the blog post. This allows you to create complex and hierarchical websites with ease.

```
pages/
├── index.js
└── blog
    ├── [slug]
    │   └── comments.js
    └── [slug].js
```

Here's an example of what the *comments.js* file might look like:

pages/blog/[slug]/comments.js

```
import { useRouter } from 'next/router';

function BlogPostComments() {
  const router = useRouter();
  const { slug } = router.query;

  return (
    <div>
      <h1>Comments for Blog Post: {slug}</h1>
      <p>This is the comments page for the blog post with the slug {slug}.</p>
    </div>
  );
}

export default BlogPostComments;
```

If a user visits the URL */blog/my-first-post/comments*, Next.js will automatically route them to the *comments.js* page inside the *[slug]* directory and set the slug parameter to *my-first-post*. The

BlogPostComments component will then be rendered with the correct *slug* parameter and display the comments for that blog post.

API Routes

Next.js also allows you to create API routes, which can be used to fetch data from your backend or third-party APIs.

API routes are similar to regular routes, but instead of returning HTML, they return data in JSON format. This makes it easy to create powerful and flexible APIs that can be used by your front end or other applications.

Let's say you have a backend API that returns a list of products in JSON format. You want to create a front-end page that displays this list of products using Next.js. To do this, you can create an API route in Next.js that fetches the data from your backend API and returns it in JSON format.

To create an API route in Next.js, you would create a file in the *pages/api* directory.

```
pages/
└── api
    └── products.js
```

Here's an example of what the *products.js* file might look like:

pages/api/products.js

```
export default async function handler(req, res) {
  const response = await fetch('https://an-external-api.com/products');
  const products = await response.json();

  res.status(200).json(products);
}
```

In this example, we're using the built-in fetch function to fetch the list of products from our backend API, and then return the list of products in JSON format using the *res.json()* method.

Now, we can use this API route to fetch the list of products from our front-end React page. Here's an example of what the front-end page might look like:

```
import { useState, useEffect } from 'react';

function ProductList() {
  const [products, setProducts] = useState([]);

  useEffect(() => {
    const fetchData = async () => {
      try {
        const response = await fetch('/api/products');
        const products = await response.json();
        setProducts(products);
      } catch (error) {
        console.error('Error fetching data:', error);
      }
    };

    fetchData();
  }, []);

  return (
    <div>
      <h1>Product List</h1>
      <ul>
        {products.map((product) => (
          <li key={product.id}>{product.name}</li>
        ))}
      </ul>
    </div>
  );
}

export default ProductList;
```

In this example, we're using the built-in fetch function to fetch the list of products from our API route, and then using the *useState* and *useEffect* hooks to update the component state with the list of products.

Now, when a user visits this page, Next.js will automatically fetch the list of products from the API route and display it on the page.

Link Component

Next.js provides a *Link* component that makes it easy to create links between pages on your website. This component uses client-side rendering to navigate between pages, which can provide a faster and smoother user experience compared to traditional page reloads.

Here's an example of how to use the *Link* component in Next.js:

```
import Link from 'next/link';

function MyComponent() {
  return (
    <div>
      <h1>My Component</h1>
      <Link href="/about">
```

```
        <a>About</a>
      </Link>
    </div>
  );
}

export default MyComponent;
```

In this example, we have a simple component that includes a link to the *about* page using the *Link* component. We provide the page URL as a prop to the *Link* component and wrap the link text in an anchor tag. Next.js automatically handles the client-side rendering for the link, providing a smooth and seamless user experience.

Conclusion

With all the features we have mentioned in this chapter, the file directory of a Next.js app might look like the following:

```
├── pages/
│   ├── index.js
│   ├── blog/
│   │   ├── index.js
│   │   ├── [slug].js
│   │   └── category/
│   │       ├── [category].js
│   │       └── index.js
│   ├── api/
│   │   └── blog/
│   │       ├── index.js
│   │       ├── [slug].js
│   │       └── category/
│   │           ├── [category].js
│   │           └── index.js
│   └── ...other pages
├── public/
│   ├── images/
│   │   └── ...images
│   └── ...other public assets
├── styles/
│   └── ...CSS files
├── components/
│   └── ...React components
├── next.config.js
├── package.json
└── ...other files and directories
```

Familiarize yourself with this file structure for future use.

While this chapter does not provide any coding examples for you to play with, don't worry, we will provide projects in future chapters that allow you to apply the concepts you've learned about Next.js.

With both React and Next.js powering the client and server-side rendering, we are still missing one thing to make a website presentable to users: styles. This is how Tailwind CSS comes into the picture.

Let's talk about Tailwind CSS now!

CHAPTER 3: INTRODUCTION TO TAILWIND CSS

What is Tailwind CSS?

Tailwind CSS is an open-source CSS framework, which includes a huge list of utility CSS classes that can be used to style each element by mixing and matching. These classes may be about colors, padding, font sizes, etc.

Let me talk about: the history of Tailwind CSS[2]

Tailwind CSS was created by Adam Wathan and Steve Schoger in 2017. While building a web app for sharing interesting articles with their team, Wathan, who was a fan of Bootstrap, began adding utility classes such as paddings and flexbox containers.

When the article-sharing app didn't pan out, the two shifted to another project. However, Wathan found himself going back to the old project and copying the utility classes over to the new one. As more people requested the utility classes, Wathan and Schoger extracted them into a library and eventually open-sourced them.

Tailwind vs. Bootstrap

If you are familiar with the CSS framework Bootstrap, you may know that the styles defined in Bootstrap are component-based, for example, buttons or tables. Compared with Bootstrap, Tailwind provides you with the freedom to create custom designs and components easily.

---

[2] The Story of Tailwind CSS feat. Adam Wathan: https://www.offerzen.com/blog/adam-wathan-story-tailwind-css

For example, to build a button component in Bootstrap, the HTML code looks like this:

HTML

```
<button class="btn btn-primary">
  Click me
</button>
```

If using Tailwind, it will look like this:

HTML

```
<button class="bg-blue-500 hover:bg-blue-700 text-white font-bold py-2 px-4 rounded">
  Click me
</button>
```

Although Bootstrap styles, such as *btn-primary*, are simpler, they lack flexibility as customization requires creating custom classes. Additionally, knowledge of specific CSS properties is necessary for creating these custom classes.

For example, To change the button text color to black, which is not preset in Bootstrap, you need to create a new class in the stylesheet as shown below, and apply it to the respective element.

CSS

```
.btn-text-black {
  color: #000000;
}
```

HTML

```
<button class="btn btn-primary btn-text-black">
  Click me
</button>
```

On the other hand, Tailwind takes a standardized approach by providing features like *bg-blue-500* for background, *hover:bg-blue-700* for mouseover effects, *text-white* for text color, and more. This allows for freedom in creating unique styles tailored to individual needs, without the need to worry about specific CSS properties.

For the example that requires a button with black text, there is no need to define a new style. Instead, simply replace "*text-white*" with "*text-black*" as follows.

HTML

```html
<button class="bg-blue-500 hover:bg-blue-700 text-black font-bold py-2 px-4 rounded">
  Click me
</button>
```

In other words, Tailwind acts as an abstraction layer for CSS properties, making it more convenient to create custom styles.

Despite being 7 years younger, Tailwind has caught up with Bootstrap in terms of daily downloads as of 2023[3], as shown in Figure 3-1.

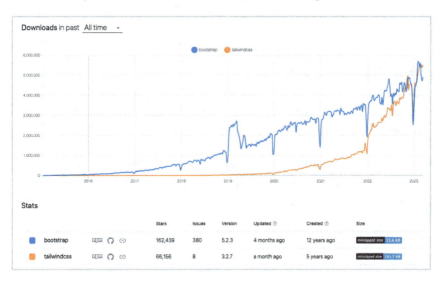

Figure 3-1: NPM Trends: Bootstrap vs. Tailwind CSS

Understanding Utility Classes

Utility classes are a core concept in Tailwind CSS, and understanding how they work is crucial for using the framework effectively.

What Are Utility Classes?

---

[3] NPM Trends Comparison between Bootstrap and Tailwind CSS:
https://npmtrends.com/bootstrap-vs-tailwindcss

In traditional CSS, styles are defined using class names that represent specific elements or groups of elements. For instance, you might use the class name *btn* to style all buttons on a page. However, this approach can lead to bloated and repetitive CSS code, especially as the number of styles and elements increases.

In contrast, utility classes are small, single-purpose classes designed to perform specific styling tasks. For example, instead of using a class like *btn* to style buttons, you might use a utility class like *bg-blue-500* to set the background color of a button to a specific shade of blue.

Tailwind CSS offers an extensive collection of utility classes that cater to a wide range of styling needs. By utilizing these classes, developers can create complex layouts and designs without writing any custom CSS code.

How Utility Classes Work in Tailwind CSS

In Tailwind CSS, utility classes are generated using a set of predefined CSS rules. These rules define specific styles for each utility class, such as font size, padding, or background color.

To use a utility class in your HTML code, you simply add the class name to the element you want to style. For example, to set the background color of a button to blue, you would add the *bg-blue-500* class to the button element:

```
<button class="bg-blue-500 text-white font-bold py-2 px-4 rounded">
  Click me!
</button>
```

In this example, the *bg-blue-500* class sets the background color to a specific shade of blue, while other utility classes like *text-white*, *font-bold*, *py-2*, *px-4*, and *rounded* set other styles like font color, font weight, padding, and border radius.

By using utility classes in this way, you can create highly customized and responsive designs without writing any custom CSS code. Tailwind CSS's extensive collection of utility classes makes it easy to create complex layouts and designs while maintaining a clean and efficient codebase.

Styling Elements with Tailwind CSS

Let's explore how to use Tailwind CSS to style various HTML elements.

Basic Styling

To apply basic styling to an element, we can use utility classes such as *bg-*, *text-*, *font-*, and *border-*. For example, to apply a blue background color to an *<div>* element, we can use the *bg-blue-500* class:

```
<div class="bg-blue-500">This div has a blue background</div>
```

Similarly, to set the text color to white and the font size to 16 pixels, we can use the *text-white* and *text-base* classes:

```
<p class="text-white text-base">This paragraph has white text and a font
size of 16px</p>
```

Padding and Margin

Tailwind CSS also provides utility classes for adjusting padding and margin. The *p-* class sets the padding of an element, while the *m-* class sets the margin. The numbers after the *p-* or *m-* class determine the size of the padding or margin. For example, to add 4 units of padding to an *<div>* element, we can use the *p-4* class:

```
<div class="p-4">This div has 4 units of padding</div>
```

Similarly, to add 2 units of margin to a paragraph element, we can use the *m-2* class:

```
<p class="m-2">This paragraph has 2 units of margin</p>
```

Display and Positioning

Tailwind CSS provides utility classes for adjusting the display and positioning of elements. For example, to make an element display as a flex container, we can use the *flex* class:

```
<div class="flex">This div is a flex container</div>
```

Similarly, to position an element absolutely at the top right of its parent element, we can use the *absolute top-0 right-0* classes:

```
<div class="absolute top-0 right-0">This div is positioned absolutely at the
top right</div>
```

Common Utility Classes

Tailwind CSS provides a comprehensive set of utility classes that allow developers to rapidly prototype and customize their user interfaces.

Let's explore some of the most popular utility classes that Tailwind CSS offers.

Layout

- *container*: Centers the content of a container element and sets a *max-width* based on the screen size.

- *mx-auto*: Sets the horizontal margin to *auto,* centering an element within its parent container.

- *flex*: Turns an element into a flex container.

- *flex-row*: Sets the *flex-direction* to *row*.

- *flex-col*: Sets the *flex-direction* to *column*.

- *justify-start*: Sets the *justify-content* property to *flex-start*.

- *justify-end*: Sets the *justify-content* property to *flex-end*.

- *justify-center*: Sets the *justify-content* property to *center*.

- *items-start*: Sets the *align-items* property to *flex-start*.

- *items-end*: Sets the *align-items* property to *flex-end*.

- *items-center*: Sets the *align-items* property to *center*.

Typography

- *text-center*: Centers the text horizontally.

- *text-left*: Aligns the text to the left.

- *text-right*: Aligns the text to the right.

- *text-justify*: Justifies the text.

- *font-bold*: Sets the font weight to bold.

- *font-medium*: Sets the font weight to medium.

- *font-normal*: Sets the font weight to normal.

- *text-sm*: Sets the font size to small.

- *text-base*: Sets the font size to base.

- *text-lg*: Sets the font size to large.

- *text-xl*: Sets the font size to extra large.

- *text-2xl*: Sets the font size to 2 times extra large.

- *text-gray-500*: Sets the text color to a specific shade of gray.

Colors

- *bg-gray-100*: Sets the background color to a specific shade of gray.

- *bg-red-500*: Sets the background color to a specific shade of red.

- *text-gray-500*: Sets the text color to a specific shade of gray.

- *text-red-500*: Sets the text color to a specific shade of red.

- *border-gray-500*: Sets the border color to a specific shade of gray.

- *border-red-500*: Sets the border color to a specific shade of red.

Spacing

- *m-2*: Sets the margin to 2 units.

- *m-4*: Sets the margin to 4 units.

- *p-2*: Sets the padding to 2 units.

- *p-4*: Sets the padding to 4 units.

- *mx-2*: Sets the horizontal margin to 2 units.

- *mx-4*: Sets the horizontal margin to 4 units.

- *my-2*: Sets the vertical margin to 2 units.

- *my-4*: Sets the vertical margin to 4 units.

These are just a few examples, as Tailwind CSS offers a wide range of utility classes beyond what has been mentioned here.

In the examples above, 1 unit is equal to 0.25rem, which translates to 4px by default in common browsers. If you want to customize the sizing scale, for example, change 1 unit to 8px instead, you can modify *tailwind.config.js*.

Let me explain: tailwind.config.js

In Tailwind CSS, the *tailwind.config.js* file is the main configuration file where you can customize various aspects of the framework. This file is typically located in the root directory of your project.

Here are some of the things that you can modify in *tailwind.config.js*:

- Theme: The *theme* object in *tailwind.config.js* allows you to customize the colors, fonts, spacing, breakpoints, and more.

- Variants: You can use the *variants* object to enable or disable certain variants, such as *hover*, *focus*, *active*, or even create your custom variants.

- Plugins: Tailwind CSS provides a plugin system that allows you to extend or modify the framework's built-in functionality. You can add your custom plugins in the *plugins* array in *tailwind.config.js*.

- Purge: The *purge* object is where you define the files that Tailwind should scan for classes to include in the final CSS file. You can also exclude files or directories from the purge process.

- Prefix: The *prefix* option lets you add a custom prefix to all Tailwind classes, which can be useful when integrating Tailwind with other CSS frameworks or libraries.

- Important: The *important* option allows you to add the *!important* flag to all generated CSS classes, which can be useful for overriding specific styles.

By customizing these options in *tailwind.config.js*, you can tailor the framework to meet your specific design requirements and workflow.

Naming Convention of Utility Classes

The naming convention for utility classes in Tailwind CSS combines the category and purpose of the class name.

The first part of the class name indicates the category of the class, which can be either the property being modified (e.g., *text* for text-related classes, *bg* for background-related classes) or the general category of the class (e.g., *flex* for flexbox-related classes, *container* for container-related classes).

The second part of the class name indicates the specific purpose of the class, such as the size, color, or positioning.

For instance, the class name *text-gray-500* sets the text color to a specific shade of gray, while *p-4* sets the padding to 4 units.

A comprehensive list of utility classes can be found on the official Tailwind CSS documentation website at https://tailwindcss.com/docs/.

Responsive Design with Tailwind CSS

Responsive design is a crucial aspect of modern web development, as users access websites on a wide range of devices with varying screen sizes. Tailwind CSS makes it easy to create responsive layouts and styles using its built-in responsive utility classes.

Let's explore the responsive design capabilities of Tailwind CSS, and how to create responsive layouts using the framework.

Understanding Responsive Design

You may have noticed that a website can appear differently on a mobile device compared to a laptop (See Figure 3-2). This is because different devices have varying screen sizes, and websites need to be designed to adapt to those screen sizes to ensure optimal user experience. This process is called responsive design.

Figure 3-2: Nike's homepage as viewed on a laptop browser (left) and a mobile browser (right)

With Tailwind CSS, we can use responsive utility classes to change the styling of our elements based on the screen size.

Using Responsive Utility Classes

Tailwind CSS includes a wide range of responsive utility classes that allow us to specify different styles for different screen sizes. These classes use breakpoints, which define the different screen sizes at which the styles should be applied.

Tailwind has 5 viewport breakpoints. To define the behavior when reaching a specific breakpoint, you just need to use the proper prefix in the styles.

Breakpoint Prefix	Minimum Width	Corresponding CSS defined inside Tailwind
sm	640px	@media (min-width: 640px) { ... }
md	768px	@media (min-width: 768px) { ... }
lg	1024px	@media (min-width: 1024px) { ... }
xl	1280px	@media (min-width: 1280px) { ... }
2xl	1536px	@media (min-width: 1536px) { ... }

For example, we can use the *sm:* prefix to apply a style only on screens that are small or larger.

Here is a concrete example:

```
<div class="bg-gray-500 sm:bg-blue-500 md:bg-green-500 lg:bg-red-500 xl:bg-yellow-500">
    Hello World
</div>
```

In this example, the *bg-gray-500* class will be applied by default (see Figure 3-3), but on small screens (*sm:*), the *bg-blue-500* class will be used instead (Figure 3-4). On medium screens (*md:*), the *bg-green-500* class will be used (Figure 3-5), and so on.

Figure 3-3: The div is gray by default

Figure 3-4: The div turns blue on small screens.

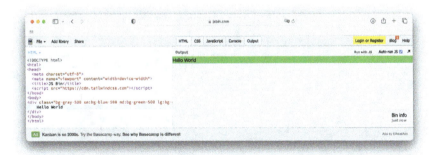

Figure 3-5: The div turns green on medium screens.

Figure 3-6: The div turns red on large screens.

Here is another example:

```
<div class="grid grid-cols-1 sm:grid-cols-2 lg:grid-cols-3">
  <div class="w-16 h-16 rounded-full bg-red-500 m-2"></div>
  <div class="w-16 h-16 rounded-full bg-red-500 m-2"></div>
  <div class="w-16 h-16 rounded-full bg-red-500 m-2"></div>
  <div class="w-16 h-16 rounded-full bg-red-500 m-2"></div>
  <div class="w-16 h-16 rounded-full bg-red-500 m-2"></div>
</div>
```

This code creates a grid of red circles. The number of columns in the grid layout changes based on the screen size, with 1 column on the default size (Figure 3-7), 2 columns on the small screens(Figure 3-9), and up to 3 columns on large screens (Figure 3-8).

Figure 3-7: The grid has only one column by default.

46

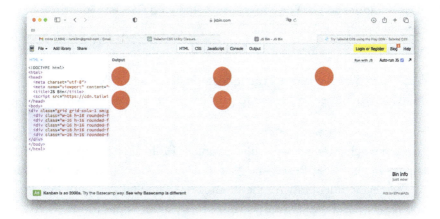

Figure 3-8: The grid has 3 columns on large screens.

Figure 3-9: The grid has 2 columns on small screens.

Conclusion

Tailwind CSS is a comprehensive and powerful tool for building modern and responsive web applications.

In this chapter, we have explored various aspects of using Tailwind CSS, including understanding utility classes, styling elements, common utility classes, and responsive design techniques. With its vast array of utility

47

classes and responsive design features, Tailwind CSS provides an excellent platform for building attractive and responsive web applications.

Now that you have learned the fundamentals of React, Next.js, and Tailwind, you must be excited to gain hands-on experience with these tools.

In the next chapter, we will build a simple "Hello World" application using Tailwind CSS, React, and Next.js. We will demonstrate how to set up the development environment, integrate Tailwind CSS with React and Next.js, and use its utility classes to style our application.

CHAPTER 4: BUILDING "HELLO WORLD"

In this chapter, we will begin by creating a basic "Hello World" application using React, Next.js, and Tailwind. This is a classic first step for learning any new software technology and is essential for understanding the fundamental concepts involved.

So grab your computer and a cup of coffee (or tea, or whatever you prefer), and let's get started on building!

Goals of this Chapter

• Lay out the foundation for forthcoming chapters about building more complex web applications

For future chapters about building other web applications, you can always refer back to this chapter for as a starting point.

The Outcome of this Chapter

1. Set up the workspace

2. Have a basic page built with React, Next.js, and Tailwind CSS served locally

Creating a Project

▷ **Open your Command Prompt, and navigate to the directory where you'd like to create the app. For example -**

```
>_ cd ~/Projects/web/
```

▶ **To create a new web app, run the following command:**

```
>_ npx create-next-app@latest next-hello-world
```

This is an interactive command. It will continue to ask you for information to initialize the app.

```
Would you like to use TypeScript with this project? › No / Yes
Would you like to use ESLint with this project? › No / Yes
Would you like to use `src/` directory with this project? › No / Yes
Would you like to use experimental `app/` directory with this project? ›
No / Yes
```

By the end of the dialogue, it will create the app and install all the dependencies, including React and Next.js.

```
Creating a new Next.js app in /Users/lehuang/Projects/web/next-hello-world.

Using npm.

Installing dependencies:
- react
- react-dom
- next
- @next/font
- typescript
- @types/react
- @types/node
- @types/react-dom
- eslint
- eslint-config-next


added 270 packages, and audited 271 packages in 13s

102 packages are looking for funding
  run `npm fund` for details

found 0 vulnerabilities

Initializing project with template: default

Initialized a git repository.

Success! Created next-hello-world at /Users/lehuang/Projects/web/next-hello-world
```

This command creates a new Next.js app in a directory called *next-hello-world*.

Navigate inside the directory, and you can see the following file structure.

```
>_ cd next-hello-world/
```

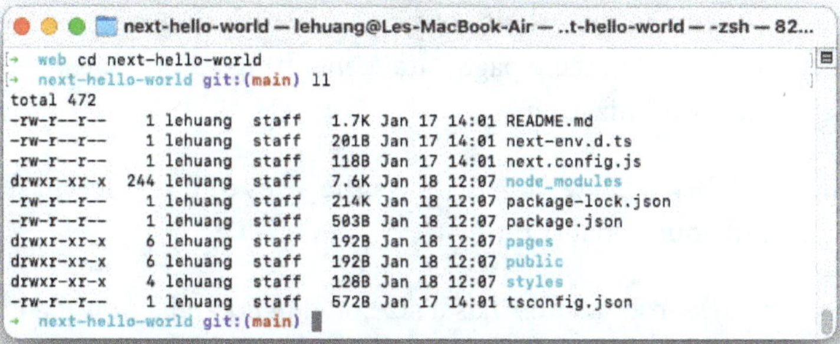

Figure 4-1: files and directories at the root of the app

Do these files and directories look familiar to you? Right, we covered them in Chapter 2. You can refer back to Chapter 2 to refresh your memory on their purpose.

▷ **Build the app.**

>_ npm run build

After the build is complete, it outputs a result similar to below.

```
> next-hello-world@0.1.0 build
> next build

info  – Linting and checking validity of types
info  – Creating an optimized production build
info  – Compiled successfully
info  – Collecting page data
info  – Generating static pages (3/3)
info  – Finalizing page optimization

Route (pages)                            Size      First Load JS
┌ ○ /                                    4.54 kB          77.6 kB
│   └ css/1beb14451460885a.css           1.86 kB
├   /_app                                0 B              73.1 kB
├ ○ /404                                 181 B            73.3 kB
└ λ /api/hello                           0 B              73.1 kB
+ First Load JS shared by all            73.8 kB
  ├ chunks/framework-2c79e2a64abdb08b.js  45.2 kB
  ├ chunks/main-f11614d8aa7ee555.js       26.8 kB
  ├ chunks/pages/_app-891652dd44e1e4e1.js 296 B
  ├ chunks/webpack-8fa1640cc84ba8fe.js    750 B
  └ css/876d048b5dab7c28.css              706 B

λ  (Server)  server-side renders at runtime (uses getInitialProps or
getServerSideProps)
○  (Static)  automatically rendered as static HTML (uses no initial props)
```

The log message shows the progress of the build process, including linting and checking the validity of types, creating an optimized production build, collecting page data, generating static pages, and finalizing page optimization.

The section labeled *Route (pages)* shows the sizes of the different pages and routes in your application.

For example, the root route / has a size of *4.54 kB* and a first load JS of *77.6 kB*. The section also shows the size of the CSS files and the shared JS files that are used by all pages.

The symbols next to each route indicate whether the page is server-side rendered (λ) or automatically rendered as static HTML (o). Server-side rendered pages are generated at runtime using *getInitialProps* or *getServerSideProps*, while statically rendered pages are generated at build time and do not require any initial props.

▷ **Start the initial web app by running the following command:**

>_ npm run start

This command is often used in the **live production environment**. It builds the application and starts a server that serves the production-ready files.

Or for convenience, you can just run this command:

>_ npm run dev

After the server starts running, it outputs a result similar to below.

```
> next-hello-world@0.1.0 dev
> next dev

ready - started server on 0.0.0.0:3000, url: http://localhost:3000
event - compiled client and server successfully in 313 ms (165 modules)
```

This command starts the **development server**. It runs the application in development mode, with features like hot reloading, which allows you to see changes made to your code without having to manually restart the server.

This makes the development process very efficient. We will continue to use this command during development.

Please note that, if you already have port 3000 used for other applications, Next.js will automatically choose to increment the port to 3001.

▷ **Open the browser and view the app at <u>http://localhost:3000</u> or <u>http://127.0.0.1:3000</u>.**

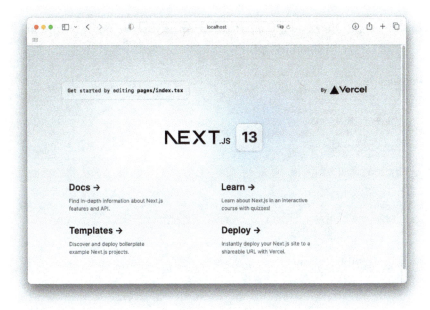

Figure 4-2: The page at <u>http://localhost:3000</u>

Let me explain: localhost and 127.0.0.1

Both *localhost* and *127.0.0.1* are commonly used to refer to the loopback address or the current machine in networking and computer systems. They are used interchangeably to access services running on the local machine or for loopback testing purposes.

localhost is a hostname that resolves to the loopback IP address, which is typically *127.0.0.1*. It is a way to refer to the current machine or the local host without using the actual IP address.

However, it's important to note that in some cases, there may be slight differences in behavior between using *localhost* and *127.0.0.1* due to how network interfaces and DNS resolution are configured on a particular system or network.

In this book, *localhost* and *127.0.0.1* can be treated as the same.

Configuring TypeScript

▷ Find the file *tsconfig.json* at the root of the project, and update the *target* in *compilerOptions* to *ES6*.

<u>tsconfig.json</u>

```json
{
  "compilerOptions": {
    "target": "es6",
    "lib": ["dom", "dom.iterable", "esnext"],
    "allowJs": true,
    "skipLibCheck": true,
    "strict": true,
    "forceConsistentCasingInFileNames": true,
    "noEmit": true,
    "esModuleInterop": true,
    "module": "esnext",
    "moduleResolution": "node",
    "resolveJsonModule": true,
    "isolatedModules": true,
    "jsx": "preserve",
    "incremental": true,
    "baseUrl": ".",
    "paths": {
      "@/*": ["./*"]
    }
  },
  "include": ["next-env.d.ts", "**/*.ts", "**/*.tsx"],
  "exclude": ["node_modules"]
}
```

Let me explain: what is TypeScript?

TypeScript is a strongly typed programming language that builds on JavaScript, which is a well-known loosely typed language. It enables developers to add type safety to their projects.

Let me explain: what is target?

Target means which version of JavaScript you using for coding. Modern browsers support all ES6 features, so ES6 is a good choice.

If you code for older systems, you may consider lower targets.

Setting Up Tailwind CSS

Now we have React and Next.js via the creation process, we need to set up Tailwind as well.

▷ **Install Tailwind CSS to the app**

Inside the app directory, run the following command:

```
>_ npm install -D tailwindcss postcss autoprefixer
```

The NPM package *tailwindcss* is exactly what its name implies: Tailwind CSS.

The package *postcss* is a module for processing and transforming styles: adding vendor prefixes, minifying CSS, and transforming modern CSS syntax into an older, browser-compatible syntax.

The package *autoprefixer* is a module for adding vendor prefixes to CSS styles, to ensure cross-browser compatibility.

Vendor prefixes are special styles that are added to certain CSS properties to ensure compatibility with specific browsers, such as Webkit, Mozilla, and Microsoft.

▷ **Create Tailwind configs in the app**

```
>_ npx tailwindcss init -p
```

This command will produce two config files: *postcss.config.js* and *tailwind.config.js*.

▷ **Update *tailwind.config.js* to configure your template paths**

tailwind.config.js
```
/** @type {import('tailwindcss').Config} */
module.exports = {
  content: [
    "./pages/**/*.{js,ts,jsx,tsx}",
```

```
    "./components/**/*.{js,ts,jsx,tsx}",
  ],
  theme: {
    extend: {},
  },
  plugins: [],
}
```

The *content* section of the *tailwind.config.js* file is where you specify the locations of all of your HTML templates, JavaScript components, and any other source files that contain Tailwind class names.

In the projects covered in this book, we will create pages and components within the two directories, specifically *./pages/* and *./components/*.

▷ **Add the following Tailwind directives to the "styles/globals.css" file, replacing its current content.**

<u>styles/globals.css</u>

```
@tailwind base;
@tailwind components;
@tailwind utilities;
```

Initially, you may notice that *globals.css* is not empty. Given that we don't need the existing styles defined in the file, we can directly replace the content with the code above.

▷ **Update the Home page.**

Replace the original *pages/index.tsx* with the content below.

<u>pages/index.tsx</u>

```
export default function Home() {
  return (
    <div className="flex h-screen w-screen items-center justify-center">
      <p className="text-bold">Hello World!</p>
    </div>
  )
}
```

This component describes what elements the home page has.

Here *.flex, .items-center, .h-screen,* and *.w-screen* are utility classes of Tailwind CSS.

h-screen and *w-screen* will set the height and width of the element to *100vh* and *100vw* respectively.

items-center and *justify-center* will align the items inside the flex container to center in both horizontal and vertical axis respectively.

flex will make the *div* act as a flex container.

Let me explain: why "className", not "class"?

You may notice something interesting in the React markup above: the *className* attribute. In HTML, *class* is used for styles. Why use *className* here in React?

The term "*class*" is a reserved keyword in JavaScript, which is used to define object-oriented classes. By using "*className*" instead, React ensures that there are no conflicts with the JavaScript language and provides a clear way of defining HTML class attributes in JSX syntax.

▷ **Start your app, if it is not running**

>_ npm run dev

▷ **Test whether Tailwind is working correctly at <u>http:// localhost:3000</u>, see Figure 4-3.**

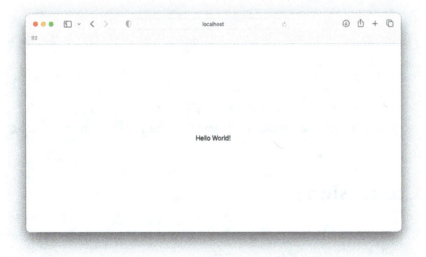

Figure 4-3: The page at <u>http://localhost:3000</u>

Excellent! We've successfully created a working web app. It is simple at the moment, but it has laid a great foundation for future chapters!

Code Example

You can always get the source code for this project at https:// github.com/higracehuang/next-hello-world.

After checking out the code, here are a few steps to make it run locally:

▷ **Install the NPM modules by running the following in the project's root directory.**

>_ `npm install`

This will install all the NPM modules based on package.json.

▷ **Build the app.**

>_ `npm run build`

▷ **Start the development server.**

>_ `npm run dev`

Or

>_ `npm run start`

▷ **Open your web browser and navigate to the appropriate URL (e.g., http://localhost:3000) to view the locally running project.**

Conclusion

In this chapter, we went through how to create a Next.js project and set up Tailwind CSS in the project.

This *Hello World* project seems small, but it is the starter for many projects later in the book.

Ready for the next challenge?

CHAPTER 5: BUILDING A PERSONAL WEBSITE

Now that we have a basic app setup, we can start to build exciting things on top of that.

A personal website serves as a platform to showcase one's experiences, achievements, ideas, and professional work, establishing a strong online presence. Let's build one!

Goals of this Chapter

By building a personal website, we will learn a lot about the many aspects:

• Next.js routing

• Server-side rendering

• React component creation

• Tailwind styling

• Responsive design with Tailwind

• Optimizing SEO with Next.js

As personal websites typically contain static content, this chapter does not focus on building interactive web apps. We will cover dynamic and interactive web development in future chapters.

Requirements of the Web App

The following features are intended to be implemented for the personal website:

- Have the following pages: *About Me, Projects,* and *Essays*

  - *About Me*: A brief self-introduction and links to social media profiles

  - *Projects*: Showcase completed and ongoing projects

  - *Essays*: Display a list of written articles

- A consistent navigation that links to all pages on the website.

- SEO optimization for better visibility and reach.

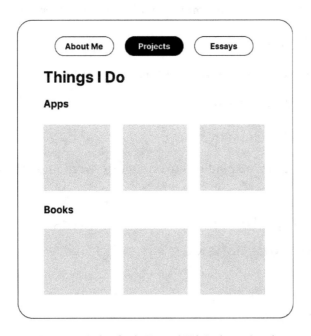

Figure 5-1: Mockup for the Personal Website (approximate)

Setting Up

For the project setup, please refer to Chapter 4.

The process can be summarized as follows:

▷ Navigate to the directory where you'd like to create the app.

```
>_ cd ~/Projects/web/
```

▷ Create a new Next.js web app with the name: *next-personal-website*.

```
>_ npx create-next-app@latest next-personal-website
```

▷ Navigate inside the *app* directory.

```
>_ cd next-personal-website/
```

▷ Configure TypeScript *target complierOptions* to *es6* in *tsconfig.json*.

▷ **Install Tailwind CSS.**

```
>_ npm install -D tailwindcss postcss autoprefixer
```

▷ **Create Tailwind configs.**

```
>_ npx tailwindcss init -p
```

▷ Update tailwind.config.js to configure your template paths.

tailwind.config.js

```
/** @type {import('tailwindcss').Config} */
module.exports = {
  content: [
    "./pages/**/*.{js,ts,jsx,tsx}",
    "./components/**/*.{js,ts,jsx,tsx}",
  ],
  theme: {
    extend: {},
  },
  plugins: [],
}
```

▷ Add the Tailwind directives to *styles/globals.css*.

styles/globals.css

```
@tailwind base;
@tailwind components;
@tailwind utilities;
```

▷ Clean up the *Home* page.

pages/index.tsx

```
export default function Home() {
  return (
    <></>
  )
}
```

▷ **Start the app.**

>_ npm run dev

▷ **Test whether Tailwind is working correctly at** http://
localhost:3000.

Creating the Pages

We will use the original *Home* page as the *About Me* page. We will create
two other pages, the *Projects* page and the *Essays* page, in the directory
pages/.

▷ **Create a new TSX file called *projects.tsx* that exports a React**
component for the *Projects* page.

pages/projects.tsx
```
export default function Projects() {
    return <div>Projects</div>
}
```

▷ **Create a new TSX file called *essays.tsx* that exports a React**
component for the *Essays* page.

pages/essays.tsx
```
export default function Essays() {
    return <div>Essays</div>
}
```

▷ **Update the existing *index.tsx* to be the page for the *About Me***
page.

pages/index.tsx
```
export default function Home() {
    return <div>About Me</div>
}
```

▷ **Test whether you can view these pages.**

On the browser, go to http://localhost:3000/, and you should be able to see the page like in Figure 5-2.

Figure 5-2: The page at http://localhost:3000

Go to http://localhost:3000/projects, and you should be able to see the page like in Figure 5-3.

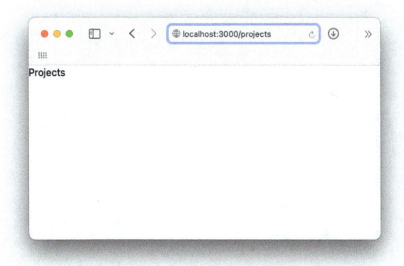

Figure 5-3: The page at http://localhost:3000/projects

Go to http://localhost:3000/essays, and you should be able to see the page like in Figure 5-4.

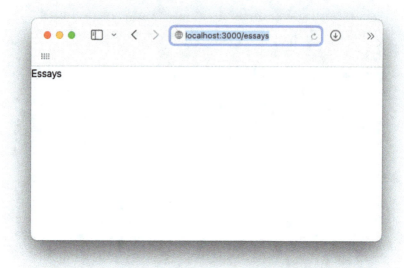

Figure 5-4: The page at http://localhost:3000/essays

Note that, when these pages are being loaded, in the Command Prompt, you can see the pages are being compiled and served, as shown in Figure 5-5.

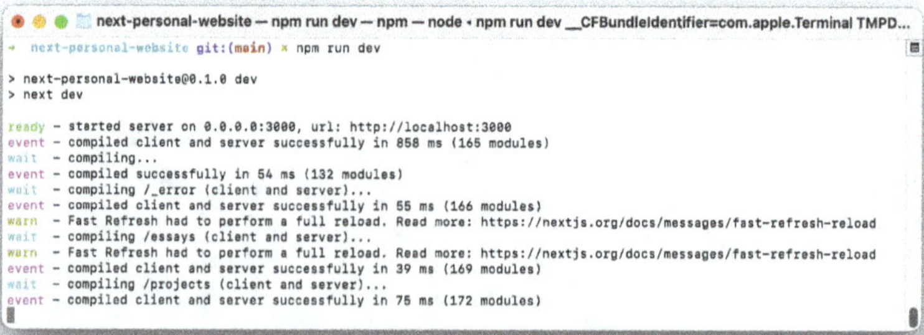

Figure 5-5: The server log in Command Prompt

Creating A Layout

To prepare for adding the navigation bar, we will ensure that all the pages adopt the same layout. Later, we can incorporate the navigation bar into the layout, so that it is applied to each of the 3 pages.

▷ **Create a TSX file called** *layout.tsx* **in the directory** *components/*.

If the directory components do not exist, create one.

▷ **Create a layout component in the file.**

components/layout.tsx

```
export default function Layout({ children }: any) {
  return (
    <>
      <main>{children}</main>
    </>
  )
}
```

Currently, the layout is almost empty. The only addition is the *<main>* tag.

Let me explain: the <main> tag

The <main> tag is a standard HTML element. It specifies the main content of a document. The content inside the <main> element should be unique to the document. It should not contain any content that is repeated across documents such as sidebars, navigation links, copyright information, site logos, and search forms.

▷ **Update** *pages/_app.tsx* **to include the layout component, whenever a page is loaded.**

pages/_app.tsx

```
import '@/styles/globals.css'
import type { AppProps } from 'next/app'
import Layout from '../components/layout'

export default function App({ Component, pageProps }: AppProps) {
  return (
    <Layout>
      <Component {...pageProps} />
    </Layout>
  )
}
```

▷ **Check the browser, and verify all 3 pages have no visual changes.**

Creating Navigation Bar

To make a navigation bar, we will build two components: *Navbar* and *NavItem*. The *NavBar* will have multiple *NavItem* components inside it.

Figure 5-6: How a navigation bar is structured with components

▷ **Create a new component *Navbar* with just one link.**

components/layout.tsx

```
function Navbar() {
  return (
    <div className="flex justify-center mx-auto max-w-7xl h-16 pt-6">
      <nav>
        <ul className="flex rounded-full bg-white/90 px-3 text-sm font-
medium text-zinc-800 shadow-lg shadow-zinc-800/5 ring-1 ring-zinc-900/5
backdrop-blur">
          <li>
            <a className="block px-3 py-2 transition hover:text-teal-500"
href="/">About Me</a>
          </li>
        </ul>
      </nav>
    </div>
  )
}

export default function Layout({ children }: any) {
  return (
    <>
      <Navbar />
      <main>{children}</main>
    </>
  )
}
```

▷ **Verify the changes in the browser, at http://localhost:3000.**

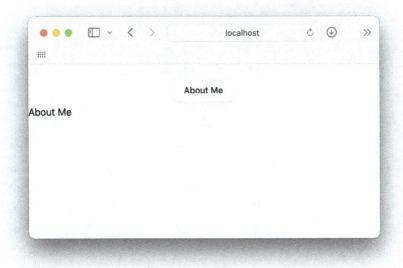

Figure 5-7: The page at http://localhost:3000

▶ Create a new component called *NavItem*, so it can be reused for all the items later.

<u>components/layout.tsx</u>

```
function NavItem() {
  return (
    <li>
      <a className="block px-3 py-2 transition hover:text-teal-500"
href="/">About Me</a>
    </li>
  )
}

function Navbar() {
  return (
    <div className="flex justify-center mx-auto max-w-7xl h-16 pt-6">
      <nav>
        <ul className="flex rounded-full bg-white/90 px-3 text-sm font-
medium text-zinc-800 shadow-lg shadow-zinc-800/5 ring-1 ring-zinc-900/5
backdrop-blur">
          <NavItem />
          <NavItem />
          <NavItem />
        </ul>
      </nav>
    </div>
  )
}

export default function Layout({ children }: any) {
  return (
    <>
```

```
      <Navbar />
      <main>{children}</main>
    </>
  )
}
```

▷ Verify the changes in the browser, at http://localhost:3000.

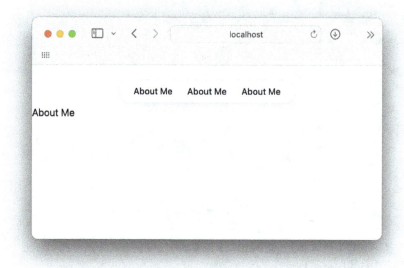

Figure 5-8: The page at http://localhost:3000

▷ Customize the *NavItem* for each page, by passing props to it.

```
type NavItemProps = {
  title: string
  url: string
}

function NavItem(props: NavItemProps) {
  const {title, url} = props
  return (
    <li>
      <a className="block px-3 py-2 transition hover:text-teal-500"
href={url}>{title}</a>
    </li>
  )
}

function Navbar() {
  return (
    <div className="flex justify-center mx-auto max-w-7xl h-16 pt-6">
      <nav>
        <ul className="flex rounded-full bg-white/90 px-3 text-sm font-
medium text-zinc-800 shadow-lg shadow-zinc-800/5 ring-1 ring-zinc-900/5
backdrop-blur">
          <NavItem title={"About Me"} url={"/"} />
```

```
          <NavItem title={"Projects"} url={"/projects"} />
          <NavItem title={"Essays"} url={"/essays"} />
        </ul>
      </nav>
    </div>
  )
}

export default function Layout({ children }: any) {
  return (
    <>
      <Navbar />
      <main>{children}</main>
    </>
  )
}
```

Alternatively, we can destructure the properties in the arguments of the *NavItem* component for brevity. The *NavItemProps* object is directly destructured to retrieve the properties *title* and *url*. This approach is equivalent to the previous syntax and simplifies the code:

```
type NavItemProps = {
  title: string
  url: string
}

function NavItem({title, url}: NavItemProps) {
  return (
    <li>
      <a className="block px-3 py-2 transition hover:text-teal-500"
href={url}>{title}</a>
    </li>
  )
}
```

Let me explain: Argument Destructuring

Argument destructuring is a technique in JavaScript that allows you to extract values from an object or an array and assign them to variables with the same name as the property being extracted. This technique makes it easier to work with complex data structures by providing a concise way to access and use their values.

Here's an example of object destructuring:

```
const person = {
  name: 'John',
  age: 30,
  address: {
    street: '123 Main St',
    city: 'Anytown',
    state: 'CA'
  }
}

const { name, age, address: { street, city, state } } = person;
```

71

```
console.log(name); // "John"
console.log(street); // "123 Main St"
console.log(state); // "CA"
```

In this example, the values of the *name, age, street, city,* and *state* properties are extracted from the *person* object and assigned to variables with the same names.

Array destructuring works similarly, but the values are extracted from an array instead of an object.

Here's an example of array destructuring:

```
const numbers = [1, 2, 3];

const [a, b, c] = numbers;

console.log(a); // 1
console.log(b); // 2
console.log(c); // 3
```

The values of the first three elements in the *numbers* array are extracted and assigned to the variables *a, b,* and *c* respectively.

Argument destructuring was introduced in ECMAScript 6 (also known as ES6 or ECMAScript 2015), which was released in June 2015. It is a feature of modern JavaScript and is widely supported by modern browsers and Node.js.

▷ **Verify the changes in the browser. Click through the tabs and verify the pages change accordingly.**

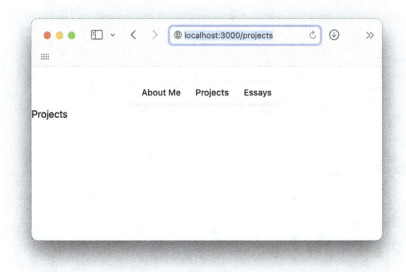

Figure 5-9: The page at http://localhost:3000/projects

Making the Navigation Bar Dynamic

At this point, the navigation bar is still static, meaning, no matter what page you are on, the navigation bar is the same.

We'd like to make it more dynamic: highlight the item when a specific page is on. Therefore, we need to pass page identification to the layout and the layout can decide how to highlight.

▷ **Pass the page identification *pageId* to the layout by using static props.**

pages/index.tsx
```
export async function getStaticProps() {
  return {
    props: {
      pageId: "about_me"
    }
  }
}

export default function Home() {
```

```
  return (
    <>About Me</>
  )
}
```

pages/essays.tsx

```
export async function getStaticProps() {
  return {
    props: {
      pageId: "essays"
    }
  }
}

export default function Essays() {
  return <div>Essays</div>
}
```

pages/projects.tsx

```
export async function getStaticProps() {
  return {
    props: {
      pageId: "projects"
    }
  }
}

export default function Projects() {
  return <div>Projects</div>
}
```

As mentioned in Chapter 2, *getStaticProps()* is a Next.js function that allows you to fetch data at build time and pass it as props to your React components. This method tells the component to populate those props and render them into a static HTML page at build time, rather than at the run time.

In the code snippet, a variable called *pageId* is created to identify each page. It is set to a string value in the *getStaticProps()* function. This value can be used to conditionally render different content or to customize the behavior of the component based on the specific page it is being rendered on.

▶ Pass the *pageId* to the layout as part of the children.props.

components/layout.tsx (Partial)

```
export default function Layout({ children }: any) {
  return (
    <>
      <Navbar pageId={children.props.pageId} />
      <main>{children}</main>
    </>
```

```
  )
}
```

➤ Pass *pageId* to the component *Navbar,* by updating the
  component *Navbar* to take an argument.

components/layout.tsx (Partial)

```
type NavbarProps = {
  pageId: string
}

function Navbar(props: NavbarProps) {
  return (
    <div className="flex justify-center mx-auto max-w-7xl h-16 pt-6">
      <nav>
        <ul className="flex rounded-full bg-white/90 px-3 text-sm font-
medium text-zinc-800 shadow-lg shadow-zinc-800/5 ring-1 ring-zinc-900/5
backdrop-blur">
          <NavItem title={"About Me"} url={"/"}   />
          <NavItem title={"Projects"} url={"/projects"} />
          <NavItem title={"Essays"} url={"/essays"} />
        </ul>
      </nav>
    </div>
  )
}
```

➤ Update the *NavItemProps* to have another argument called
  isSelected.

components/layout.tsx (Partial)

```
type NavItemProps = {
  title: string
  url: string
  isSelected: boolean
}
```

➤ Update the *Navbar* to pass this new argument *isSelected.*

components/layout.tsx (Partial)

```
function Navbar(props: NavbarProps) {
  return (
    <div className="flex justify-center mx-auto max-w-7xl h-16 pt-6">
      <nav>
        <ul className="flex rounded-full bg-white/90 px-3 text-sm font-
medium text-zinc-800 shadow-lg shadow-zinc-800/5 ring-1 ring-zinc-900/5
backdrop-blur">
          <NavItem title={"About Me"} url={"/"} isSelected={props.pageId ==
"about_me"}  />
          <NavItem title={"Projects"} url={"/projects"}
isSelected={props.pageId == "projects"} />
          <NavItem title={"Essays"} url={"/essays"} isSelected={props.pageId
== "essays"} />
        </ul>
      </nav>
    </div>
  )
}
```

▶ Update the *NavItem* to use different styles based on the value of *isSelected*.

components/layout.tsx (Partial)
```
function NavItem(props: NavItemProps) {
  const {title, url, isSelected} = props
  return (
    <li>
      <a className={`block px-3 py-2 transition hover:text-teal-500 $
{isSelected ? "text-teal-500" : ""}`} href={url}>{title}</a>
    </li>
  )
}
```

▶ Verify the changes in the browser.

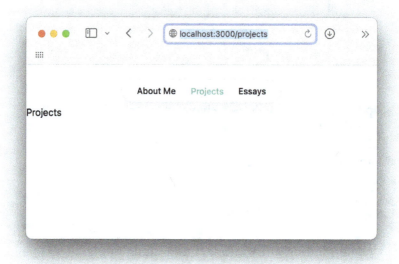

Figure 5-10: The page at http://localhost:3000/projects

Complete Code for the Layout Component

At this point, the navigation bar should be functional after implementing the incremental changes. The resulting output is as follows:

components/layout.tsx
```
type NavItemProps = {
```

```
    title: string
    url: string
    isSelected: boolean
}

function NavItem(props: NavItemProps) {
  const {title, url, isSelected} = props
  return (
    <li>
      <a className={`block px-3 py-2 transition hover:text-teal-500 $
{isSelected ? "text-teal-500" : ""}`} href={url}>{title}</a>
    </li>
  )
}

type NavbarProps = {
  pageId: string
}

function Navbar(props: NavbarProps) {
  return (
    <div className="flex justify-center mx-auto max-w-7xl h-16 pt-6">
      <nav>
        <ul className="flex rounded-full bg-white/90 px-3 text-sm font-
medium text-zinc-800 shadow-lg shadow-zinc-800/5 ring-1 ring-zinc-900/5
backdrop-blur">
          <NavItem title={"About Me"} url={"/"} isSelected={props.pageId ==
"about_me"} />
          <NavItem title={"Projects"} url={"/projects"}
isSelected={props.pageId == "projects"} />
          <NavItem title={"Essays"} url={"/essays"} isSelected={props.pageId
== "essays"} />
        </ul>
      </nav>
    </div>
  )
}

export default function Layout({ children }: any) {
  return (
    <>
      <Navbar pageId={children.props.pageId} />
      <main>{children}</main>
    </>
  )
}
```

Building the Footer

▷ Create a simple component called *Footer*, with no props
  initially.

components/layout.tsx (Partial)

```
function Footer() {
  return <footer></footer>
}
```

▶ **Add the *Footer* component to the Layout.**

components/layout.tsx (Partial)

```
export default function Layout({ children }: any) {
  return (
    <>
      <Navbar pageId={children.props.pageId} />
      <main>{children}</main>
      <Footer />
    </>
  )
}
```

▶ **Updating the content of the component *Footer*.**

Since all the links in the footer have the same styles, we can go even further to modularize the components, by making the link into its component called *FooterLink*.

components/layout.tsx (Partial)

```
type FooterLinkProps = {
  text: string
  url: string
}

function FooterLink(props: FooterLinkProps) {
  let {url, text} = props
  return <a className="transition hover:text-teal-500" href={url}>{text}</a>
}

function Footer() {
  return <footer className="pt-10 px-8 pb-16 border-t">
    <div className="flex justify-between gap-6">
      <div className="flex gap-6 text-sm font-medium text-zinc-600">
        <FooterLink text={"About Me"} url={"/"} />
        <FooterLink text={"Projects"} url={"/projects"} />
        <FooterLink text={"Essays"} url={"/essays"} />
      </div>
      <p className="text-sm text-zinc-400">© 2023 Grace Huang. All rights reserved.</p>
    </div>
  </footer>
}
```

▶ **Verify the UI in the browser.**

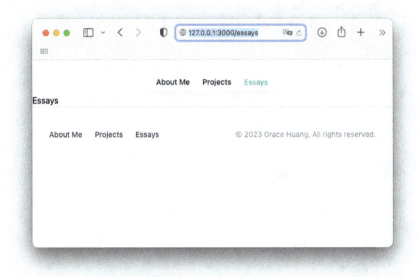

Figure 5-11: The page at The page at http://localhost:3000/essays

Next, we'll start creating each page, but to keep things fun and fresh, we'll focus on one page - *Projects*. Later, you can apply what you've learned to build the *Essays* and *About Me* pages.

Building the Projects Page

▷ **Set up the layout for the Projects page.**

pages/projects.tsx

```
export default function Projects() {
  return <div className="mt-16 px-8">
    <header>
      <h1 className="font-bold text-4xl text-zinc-800">Things I Do</h1>
      <p className="text-base mt-6 text-zinc-600">I have been working on a
number of small creative projects</p>
    </header>
    <div className="mt-16">
      <h2 className="text-2xl">Apps</h2>
    </div>
    <div className="mt-16">
      <h2 className="text-2xl">Books</h2>
    </div>
  </div>
}
```

In the browser, the *Projects* page will look like the following:

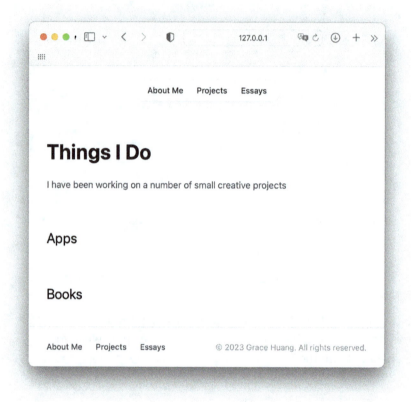

Figure 5-12: The page at http://localhost:3000/projects

▷ **Create a list in the form of a 4-column grid.**

pages/projects.tsx

```
export default function Projects() {
  return <div className="mt-16 px-8">
    <header>
      <h1 className="font-bold text-4xl text-zinc-800">Things I Do</h1>
      <p className="text-base mt-6 text-zinc-600">I have been working on a
number of small creative projects</p>
    </header>
    <div className="mt-16">
      <h2 className="text-2xl">Apps</h2>
      <ul className="grid grid-cols-4 gap-x-12 gap-y-16 mt-8">
        <li>
          <a href="[link]">
            <div className="max-w-sm rounded overflow-hidden shadow-lg">
              <div className="px-6 py-4">
                <div className="font-bold text-xl mb-2">[name]</div>
              </div>
```

80

```
                <div className="px-6 pb-4">
                    <span className="inline-block bg-gray-200 rounded-full px-3
py-1 text-sm font-semibold text-gray-700 mr-2 mb-2">🔗[URL]</span>
                </div>
            </div>
        </a>
      </li>
    </ul>
  </div>
  <div className="mt-16">
    <h2 className="text-2xl">Books</h2>
  </div>
</div>
}
```

The 4-column grid is specified by the styles *grid grid-cols-4*.

The style *gap-x-12* specifies the size of the gap between grid items horizontally. In this case, the gap is 12. You can adjust this number to your preference. The style *gap-y-16* specifies the size of the gap between them vertically, which is currently set to 16.

In the browser, the *Projects* page will look like this in Figure 5-13.

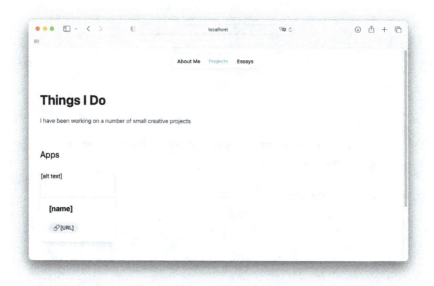

Figure 5-13: The page at http://localhost:3000/projects

You may have noticed that the name (*[name]*), the URL (*[URL]*), and the alt text (*[alt text]*) are placeholders currently. We will update them with the actual values at a later time.

You may have also noticed that currently, there is only one item in the grid. We will use this one item as a template to create a new component that can be reused for multiple items.

▷ **Extract the *<li>* and turn it into a component for a project item called *ProjectItem*.**

pages/projects.tsx (Partial)

```
type ProjectItemProps = {
  name: string
  url: string
  urlDisplay: string
}


function ProjectItem(props: ProjectItemProps) {
  let { name, url, urlDisplay, imageSrc: image } = props
  return <li>
    <a href={url}>
      <div className="max-w-sm rounded overflow-hidden shadow-lg">
        <div className="px-6 py-4">
          <div className="font-bold text-xl mb-2">{name}</div>
        </div>
        <div className="px-6 pb-4">
          <span className="inline-block bg-gray-200 rounded-full px-3 py-1
text-sm font-semibold text-gray-700 mr-2 mb-2">⌕{urlDisplay}</span>
        </div>
      </div>
    </a>
  </li>
}
```

▷ **Update the *Projects* page to use the *ProjectItem* component to populate the items in the grid.**

pages/projects.tsx (Partial)

```
export default function Projects() {
  return <div className="mt-16 px-8">
    <header>
      <h1 className="font-bold text-4xl text-zinc-800">Things I Do</h1>
      <p className="text-base mt-6 text-zinc-600">I have been working on a
number of small creative projects</p>
    </header>
    <div className="mt-16">
      <h2 className="text-2xl">Apps</h2>
      <ul className="grid grid-cols-4 gap-x-12 gap-y-16 mt-8">
        <ProjectItem name={"TallyCoin: Tracking Chores And Rewards"}
url={"https://apps.apple.com/us/app/tallycoin/id1633932632"}
urlDisplay={"App Store"} />
        <ProjectItem name={"RedacApp: Redact Text In Images"} url={"https://
gracehuang.gumroad.com/l/redac"} urlDisplay={"gumroad.com"} />
      </ul>
    </div>
    <div className="mt-16">
```

```
        <h2 className="text-2xl">Books</h2>
        <ul className="grid grid-cols-4 gap-x-12 gap-y-16 mt-8">
            <ProjectItem name={"Building macOS apps with SwiftUI: A Practical
Learning Guide"} url={"https://www.amazon.com/gp/product/B0BP5P9H31"}
urlDisplay={"amazon.com"} />
            <ProjectItem name={"Nail A Coding Interview: Six-Step Mental
Framework"} url={"https://gracehuang.gumroad.com/l/coding-interview"}
urlDisplay={"gracehuang.gumroad.com"} />
            <ProjectItem name={"A Practical Guide to Writing a Software Tech
Design Doc"} url={"https://gracehuang.gumroad.com/l/mqmUt"}
urlDisplay={"gracehuang.gumroad.com"} />
            <ProjectItem name={"Code Reviews in Tech: The Missing Guide"}
url={"https://gracehuang.gumroad.com/l/codereviews"}
urlDisplay={"gracehuang.gumroad.com"} />
        </ul>
    </div>
  </div>
}
```

In the browser, the projects page will look like this in Figure 5-14.

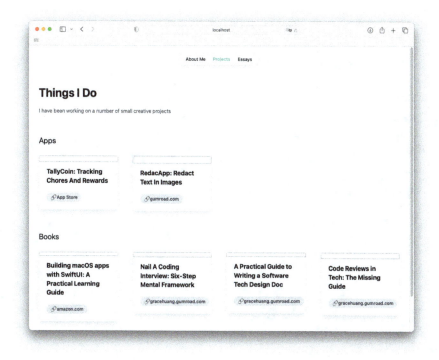

Figure 5-14: The page at http://localhost:3000/projects

▷ Import the images

We will also need the images to show on the page, so we store the images in the directory *public/images*.

83

The images can be found at https://github.com/higracehuang/next-personal-website/tree/main/public/images. Alternatively, feel free to use your own images.

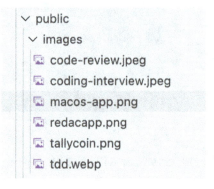

Figure 5-15: The *public/images* directory

▶ Show the images on the web page

pages/projects.tsx

```
import Image, { StaticImageData } from "next/image"

import imageBookCodingInterview from "../public/images/coding-interview.jpeg"
import imageBookCodeReview from "../public/images/code-review.jpeg"
import imageBookTDD from "../public/images/tdd.webp"
import imageAppRedacApp from "../public/images/redacapp.png"
import imageAppTallyCoin from "../public/images/tallycoin.png"
import imageBookMacOSApp from "../public/images/macos-app.png"
export async function getStaticProps() {
  return {
    props: {
      pageId: "projects"
    }
  }
}

type ProjectItemProps = {
  name: string
  url: string
  urlDisplay: string
  imageSrc: StaticImageData
}

function ProjectItem(props: ProjectItemProps) {
  let { name, url, urlDisplay, imageSrc: image } = props
  return <li>
    <a href={url}>
      <div className="max-w-sm rounded overflow-hidden shadow-lg">
        <Image className="w-full" src={image} alt={name} />
        <div className="px-6 py-4">
          <div className="font-bold text-xl mb-2">{name}</div>
```

```
        </div>
        <div className="px-6 pb-4">
          <span className="inline-block bg-gray-200 rounded-full px-3 py-1
text-sm font-semibold text-gray-700 mr-2 mb-2">🔗{urlDisplay}</span>
        </div>
      </div>
    </a>
  </li>
}

export default function Projects() {
  return <div className="mt-16 px-8">
    <header>
      <h1 className="font-bold text-4xl text-zinc-800">Things I Do</h1>
      <p className="text-base mt-6 text-zinc-600">I have been working on a
number of small creative projects</p>
    </header>
    <div className="mt-16">
      <h2 className="text-2xl">Apps</h2>
      <ul className="grid grid-cols-4 gap-x-12 gap-y-16 mt-8">
        <ProjectItem name={"TallyCoin: Tracking Chores And Rewards"}
url={"https://apps.apple.com/us/app/tallycoin/id1633932632"}
urlDisplay={"App Store"} imageSrc={imageAppTallyCoin} />
        <ProjectItem name={"RedacApp: Redact Text In Images"} url={"https://
gracehuang.gumroad.com/l/redac"} urlDisplay={"gumroad.com"}
imageSrc={imageAppRedacApp} />
      </ul>
    </div>
    <div className="mt-16">
      <h2 className="text-2xl">Books</h2>
      <ul className="grid grid-cols-4 gap-x-12 gap-y-16 mt-8">
        <ProjectItem name={"Building macOS apps with SwiftUI: A Practical
Learning Guide"} url={"https://www.amazon.com/gp/product/B0BP5P9H31"}
urlDisplay={"amazon.com"} imageSrc={imageBookMacOSApp} />
        <ProjectItem name={"Nail A Coding Interview: Six-Step Mental
Framework"} url={"https://gracehuang.gumroad.com/l/coding-interview"}
urlDisplay={"gracehuang.gumroad.com"} imageSrc={imageBookCodingInterview} />
        <ProjectItem name={"A Practical Guide to Writing a Software Tech
Design Doc"} url={"https://gracehuang.gumroad.com/l/mqmUt"}
urlDisplay={"gracehuang.gumroad.com"} imageSrc={imageBookTDD} />
        <ProjectItem name={"Code Reviews in Tech: The Missing Guide"}
url={"https://gracehuang.gumroad.com/l/codereviews"}
urlDisplay={"gracehuang.gumroad.com"} imageSrc={imageBookCodeReview} />
      </ul>
    </div>
  </div>
}
```

Instead of using the <img> tag in HTML, we use the <Image>
component from Next.js for its additional support, as mentioned in
Chapter 2.

First, the <Image> component automatically implements lazy loading,
improving page load time and performance by loading images only when
necessary.

Additionally, it can optimize images for better performance, such as by
resizing and compressing them.

Third, it can be easily configured to dynamically load images based on specific conditions, such as the device type or network speed.

In the browser, the Projects page will look like this in Figure 5-16.

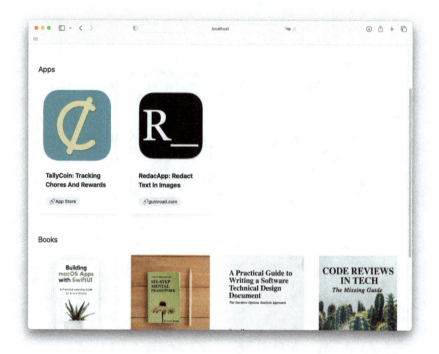

Figure 5-16: The page at http://localhost:3000/projects

▶ Make the page responsive to the screen size

Previously, the grid is set to be always with 4 columns. Obviously, it will look compressed on mobile because the screen is narrower.

We'd like the page to be responsive: the grid has fewer columns when the viewport is smaller, and more columns when the viewport is bigger. Tailwind CSS makes this job so much easier.

Now, we would like the grid to be like this: for small screens, the grid will have only 1 column. For medium screens, it will have 2 columns. For large screens, it will have 4 columns.

The style class will be *grid grid-cols-1 md:grid-cols-2 lg:grid-cols-4*. Why? Let me explain.

- The base case for all screens is 1 column (*grid-cols-1*).

- When the screen expands and reaches the breakpoint for the medium size, the grid becomes 2 (*md:grid-cols-2*).

- When the screen expands and reaches the large size, the grid becomes 4 (*lg:grid-cols-4*).

Next, let's update the markup with the style in the code.

pages/projects.tsx (Partial)

```
export default function Projects() {
  return <div className="mt-16 px-8">
    <header>
      <h1 className="font-bold text-4xl text-zinc-800">Things I Do</h1>
      <p className="text-base mt-6 text-zinc-600">I have been working on a
number of small creative projects</p>
    </header>
    <div className="mt-16">
      <h2 className="text-2xl">Apps</h2>
      <ul className="grid grid-cols-1 md:grid-cols-2 lg:grid-cols-4 gap-x-12
gap-y-16 mt-8">
        <ProjectItem name={"TallyCoin: Tracking Chores And Rewards"}
url={"https://apps.apple.com/us/app/tallycoin/id1633932632"}
urlDisplay={"App Store"} imageSrc={imageAppTallyCoin} />
        <ProjectItem name={"RedacApp: Redact Text In Images"} url={"https://
gracehuang.gumroad.com/l/redac"} urlDisplay={"gumroad.com"}
imageSrc={imageAppRedacApp} />
      </ul>
    </div>
    <div className="mt-16">
      <h2 className="text-2xl">Books</h2>
      <ul className="grid grid-cols-1 md:grid-cols-2 lg:grid-cols-4 gap-x-12
gap-y-16 mt-8">
        <ProjectItem name={"Building macOS apps with SwiftUI: A Practical
Learning Guide"} url={"https://www.amazon.com/gp/product/B0BP5P9H31"}
urlDisplay={"amazon.com"} imageSrc={imageBookMacOSApp} />
        <ProjectItem name={"Nail A Coding Interview: Six-Step Mental
Framework"} url={"https://gracehuang.gumroad.com/l/coding-interview"}
urlDisplay={"gracehuang.gumroad.com"} imageSrc={imageBookCodingInterview} />
        <ProjectItem name={"A Practical Guide to Writing a Software Tech
Design Doc"} url={"https://gracehuang.gumroad.com/l/mqmUt"}
urlDisplay={"gracehuang.gumroad.com"} imageSrc={imageBookTDD} />
        <ProjectItem name={"Code Reviews in Tech: The Missing Guide"}
url={"https://gracehuang.gumroad.com/l/codereviews"}
urlDisplay={"gracehuang.gumroad.com"} imageSrc={imageBookCodeReview} />
      </ul>
    </div>
  </div>
}
```

You can also try different configurations to see how it responds.

Complete Code of the Project Page

By now, a responsive Projects page with all the necessary information has been completed. The resulting output is as follows:

pages/projects.tsx

```tsx
import Image, { StaticImageData } from "next/image"

import imageBookCodingInterview  from "../public/images/coding-
interview.jpeg"
import imageBookCodeReview from "../public/images/code-review.jpeg"
import imageBookTDD from "../public/images/tdd.webp"
import imageAppRedacApp from "../public/images/redacapp.png"
import imageAppTallyCoin from "../public/images/tallycoin.png"
import imageBookMacOSApp from "../public/images/macos-app.png"

export async function getStaticProps() {
  return {
    props: {
      pageId: "projects"
    }
  }
}

type ProjectItemProps = {
  name: string
  url: string
  urlDisplay: string
  imageSrc: StaticImageData
}

function ProjectItem(props: ProjectItemProps) {
  let { name, url, urlDisplay, imageSrc: image } = props
  return <li>
    <a href={url}>
      <div className="max-w-sm rounded overflow-hidden shadow-lg">
        <Image className="w-full" src={image} alt={name} />
        <div className="px-6 py-4">
          <div className="font-bold text-xl mb-2">{name}</div>
        </div>
        <div className="px-6 pb-4">
          <span className="inline-block bg-gray-200 rounded-full px-3 py-1
text-sm font-semibold text-gray-700 mr-2 mb-2">🔗{urlDisplay}</span>
        </div>
      </div>
    </a>
  </li>
}

export default function Projects() {
  return <div className="mt-16 px-8">
    <header>
      <h1 className="font-bold text-4xl text-zinc-800">Things I Do</h1>
      <p className="text-base mt-6 text-zinc-600">I have been working on a
number of small creative projects</p>
    </header>
    <div className="mt-16">
      <h2 className="text-2xl">Apps</h2>
      <ul className="grid grid-cols-1 md:grid-cols-2 lg:grid-cols-4 gap-x-12
gap-y-16 mt-8">
```

```
        <ProjectItem name={"TallyCoin: Tracking Chores And Rewards"}
url={"https://apps.apple.com/us/app/tallycoin/id1633932632"}
urlDisplay={"App Store"} imageSrc={imageAppTallyCoin} />
        <ProjectItem name={"RedacApp: Redact Text In Images"} url={"https://
gracehuang.gumroad.com/l/redac"} urlDisplay={"gumroad.com"}
imageSrc={imageAppRedacApp} />
      </ul>
    </div>
    <div className="mt-16">
      <h2 className="text-2xl">Books</h2>
      <ul className="grid grid-cols-1 md:grid-cols-2 lg:grid-cols-4 gap-x-12
gap-y-16 mt-8">
        <ProjectItem name={"Building macOS apps with SwiftUI: A Practical
Learning Guide"} url={"https://www.amazon.com/gp/product/B0BP5P9H31"}
urlDisplay={"amazon.com"} imageSrc={imageBookMacOSApp} />
        <ProjectItem name={"Nail A Coding Interview: Six-Step Mental
Framework"} url={"https://gracehuang.gumroad.com/l/coding-interview"}
urlDisplay={"gracehuang.gumroad.com"} imageSrc={imageBookCodingInterview} />
        <ProjectItem name={"A Practical Guide to Writing a Software Tech
Design Doc"} url={"https://gracehuang.gumroad.com/l/mqmUt"}
urlDisplay={"gracehuang.gumroad.com"} imageSrc={imageBookTDD} />
        <ProjectItem name={"Code Reviews in Tech: The Missing Guide"}
url={"https://gracehuang.gumroad.com/l/codereviews"}
urlDisplay={"gracehuang.gumroad.com"} imageSrc={imageBookCodeReview} />
      </ul>
    </div>
  </div>
}
```

Great job! With the skills you have acquired from creating the Projects page, you now have the freedom to let your creativity flow and design the other pages, such as About Me and Essays, as you see fit.

Making the Page SEO-Friendly

Let me explain: why SEO is important

SEO, or Search Engine Optimization, is the practice of optimizing your website or application to improve its visibility and relevance to search engines, making it easier for them to understand and interpret your content.

This is crucial if your aim is to drive more traffic to your website. When people search on the internet, they are looking for something, and that something could be your business or the content you are promoting. By increasing your website's visibility in search results, you can attract more visitors, which in turn can lead to potential sales or customers for your business.

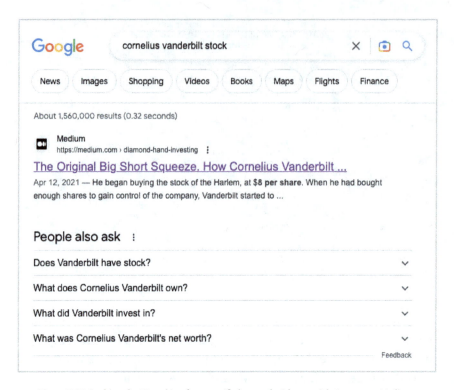

Figure 5-17: I achieved a #1 ranking for a specific keyword with an article I wrote on Medium, resulting in a substantial increase in daily traffic to the article.

In SEO, several key elements play a crucial role on a web page, including the title tag, meta description, heading tags, URL structure, content, images, and presence in social sharing.

For the project we are building, you might have noticed that something's missing on the pages, such as favicon, page titles, and social *<meta>* tags, by inspecting the HTML elements on the page.

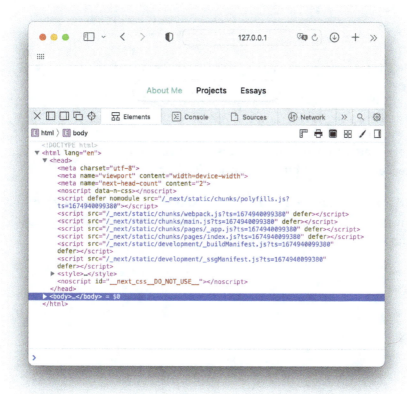

Figure 5-18: The HTML elements on the page at http://localhost:3000/projects

But don't worry! These are crucial to make sure your pages are easily discoverable on search engines, let's add them in and make sure your site is SEO-friendly.

Let me explain: how to inspect elements in browsers

You can check page HTML elements in any browser. To inspect elements in a web browser:

Right-click on the element you want to inspect and select *Inspect* or *Inspect Element*.

Use the keyboard shortcut:

- Chrome: "Ctrl + Shift + I" or "F12"

- Firefox: "Ctrl + Shift + I"

- Safari: "Cmd + Option + I"

Click the "Elements" tab in the Developer Tools panel that opens to inspect HTML and CSS.

▶ Set up the favicon on the layout

Let's start with what all the pages have in common (for example, favicon), so we can put them inside the layout.

Prepare a favicon[4] you prefer (I created one with the letter G, short for my name *Grace*, see Figure 5-19) and put it under the directory *public/*, and update the layout accordingly.

---

[4] A favicon, a small icon representing a website, plays a crucial role in establishing brand identity. It can be seen on browser tabs, in bookmarks, and in search engine results, helping to differentiate your website from others.

Figure 5-19: The look of favicon.ico

components/layout.tsx (Partial)

```
import Head from 'next/head'

...

export default function Layout({ children }: any) {
  return (
    <>
      <Head>
        <link rel="icon" href="/favicon.ico" />
      </Head>
      <Navbar pageId={children.props.pageId} />
      <main>{children}</main>
      <Footer />
    </>
  )
}
```

After you've added the lines above, check out the page in the browser. Inspect the elements on the page, and you should be able to see the <link> element has been added.

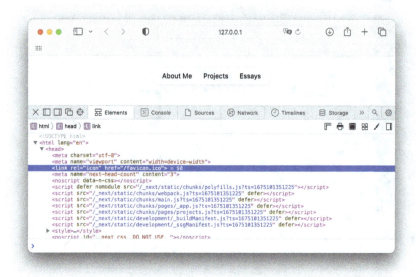

Figure 5-20: How the favicon.ico is linked on the page

▶ **Set up the title, description, and social tags for the individual pages**

Both the title and description elements are important for improving a website's SEO and can impact how easily a web page can be found through search engines.

Social tags enable social media platforms to accurately display a preview of a page's content when it is shared on their platform, including its title, description, image, and other information.

For example, this is how the link to my article[5] on Medium may be represented in a tweet:

---

[5] How A Change of CEO Either Makes Or Breaks A Company https://medium.com/@imgracehuang/how-a-change-of-ceo-either-makes-or-breaks-a-company-76c8b7412bd5

Figure 5-21: How social tags of an Medium article I wrote are presented in a tweet.

The title, description, and social tags of each page may vary based on its content, but every page will have them. So similar to *pageId* previously, we will pass individual values for metadata from the page component to the layout component via *getStaticProps()*.

Let's first start with the *About Me* page.

pages/index.tsx (Partial)

```
export async function getStaticProps() {
  return {
    props: {
      pageId: "about_me",
      metadata: {
        title: "Grace Huang",
        description: "Discover the work of Grace Huang on her personal website. ",
        openGraph: {
          image: "https://example.com/image.jpg",
```

```
            url: "https://example.com"
        }
      }
    }
  }
}

export default function Home() {
  return <div className="mt--16 px-8">
    <header>
      <h1 className="font-bold text--4xl text-zinc-800">I&apos;m Grace</h1>
    </header>
  </div>
}
```

components/layout.tsx (Partial)

```
export default function Layout({ children }: any) {
  return (
    <>
      <Head>
        <link rel="icon" href="/favicon.ico" />
        <title>{children.props.metadata.title}</title>
        <meta name="description"
content={children.props.metadata.description} />
        {/* Open Graph tags */}
        <meta property="og:title" content={children.props.metadata.title} />
        <meta property="og:description"
content={children.props.metadata.description} />
        <meta property="og:image"
content={children.props.metadata.openGraph.image} />
        <meta property="og:url"
content={children.props.metadata.openGraph.url} />
      </Head>
      <Navbar pageId={children.props.pageId} />
      <main>{children}</main>
      <Footer />
    </>
  )
}
```

After you've added the *<Head>* to the index page, you should see the
page has a title display on the tab.

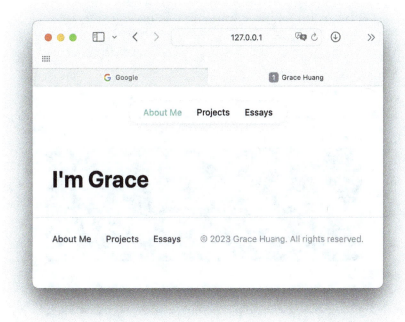

Figure 5-22: The title shows "Grace Huang" after the change in the <title> tag

With the metadata for the *About Me* page added, you can move on to the other two pages: *Projects* and *Essays*. Simply modify the *getStaticProps()* on both pages.

As the layout component now requires values for metadata, not updating the other two pages will result in errors (as shown in Figure 5-23).

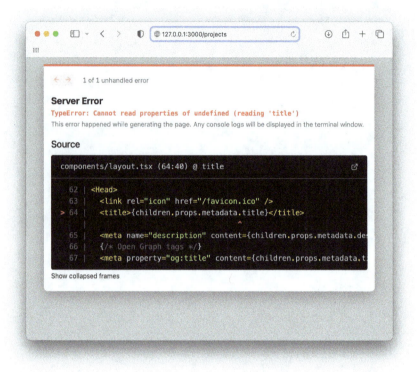

Figure 5-23: The page error after the property title is not provided

Code Example

If you feel overwhelmed by the code, don't worry! You can refer to the code example at https://github.com/higracehuang/next-personal-website for guidance.

Conclusion

In this chapter, we covered several basic and important concepts in Next.js and React.

Creating New React Components

You have built quite a few React components such as *<NavItem>* and *<ProjectItem>*. Are you familiar with the process?

The general steps are as follows:

1. Create a function for the component, with no props initially.

```
function NavItem() {
  return (
    // component markup
  );
}
```

2. Call the component from the parent component.

```
function Navbar() {
  return (
    <nav>
      <NavItem />
    </nav>
  );
}
```

3. Stub the component with static markup.

```
function NavItem() {
  return (
    <a href="#">Link</a>
  );
}
```

4. Define the props type.

```
type NavItemProps = {
  label: string,
  url: string,
};
```

5. Update the component signature to have the props, parse the props within the component, and update the markup to output the props.

```
function NavItem(props: NavItemProps) {
  return (
    <a href={props.url}>{props.label}</a>
  );
}
```

6. Update the parent component by passing different arguments to the new component.

```
function Navbar() {
  return (
    <nav>
      <NavItem label="Home" url="/" />
      <NavItem label="About" url="/about" />
      <NavItem label="Contact" url="/contact" />
```

```
    </nav>
  );
}
```

Usage of *getStaticProps()* in Next.js

getStaticProps() is a Next.js function that generates props for a page during build time, improving performance by pre-fetching data.

It creates static pages optimized for search engines, such as information in the metadata.

Responsive Design with Tailwind

Tailwind CSS provides a set of pre-defined utility classes that help developers create responsive layouts and user interfaces easily.

Great work on building a static website in this chapter! The skills you learned will serve as building blocks for the next chapter, where you'll create an even more complex app with a dynamic user interface.

CHAPTER 6: BUILDING A WEATHER APP

In this chapter, we will build some more advanced together: a weather app. Let's call it WeatherWise.

Goals of this Chapter

We will learn a lot about many aspects of a dynamic web app by building a weather web app, including:

• Interacting with external APIs to retrieve weather data

• Creating internal APIs in Next.js to manage and serve data

• Developing a user interface in React that dynamically updates based on user input, such as searching for and selecting a location.

Requirements of the Weather App

These are the features we aim to implement in the weather app:

• Search: Enable users to search for weather information for a specific city

• City name suggestions: provide users with city suggestions based on their input strings, to prevent confusion such as Paris, Texas vs. Paris, France, or Saint Petersburg, Russia vs. Saint Petersburg, Florida.

• Display: Show the high and low temperatures, as well as the weather description (e.g., rain, snow, hail) for the selected city.

Figure 6-1: A rough mock-up of the WeatherWise app.

System Design

Before delving into the code, it is efficient to start with system design for a sizable project like WeatherWise. This approach will provide a clear roadmap for determining the necessary components of the system and their sequencing.

System Diagram

A system diagram is a graphical overview of how different parts of a system interact with each other to achieve the desired functionality.

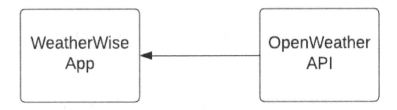

Figure 6-2: Key system components of the weather app

This diagram in Figure 6-2 outlines the key components of the system, which includes utilizing a third-party weather API in the WeatherWise app.

For educational purposes, we will be using the Weather API provided by OpenWeather. OpenWeather offers 1,000 API calls per day for free.

Sequence Diagram

A sequence diagram is useful to visualize the order of interactions between components in a system.

Here is the sequence diagram to describe WeatherWise.

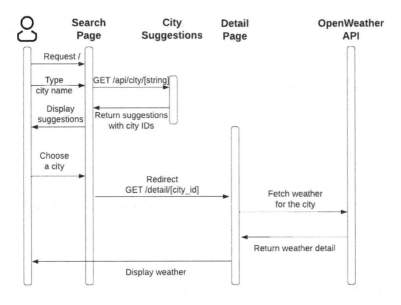

Figure 6-3: The sequence diagram of the weather app

Based on the diagram above, the flow is as follows:

1. The **user** goes to the search page by typing in the domain name in the browser, for example, https://www.weatherwise.com/.

2. The **user** types in a city name or partial city name in the search box.

3. The **search page** sends a request to the city lookup endpoint /city/ [string], for example, https://www.weatherwise.com/city/sea, to fetch the possible cities with the prefix *sea* as suggestions.

4. The **city lookup endpoint** returns a list of cities, with their city IDs.

5. The **search page** displays the list to the user.

6. The **user** chooses a city from the list.

7. The **search page** redirects to the weather detail page with the city ID in the URL parameters.

8. The **search page** sends a request to the third-party API (OpenWeather) to fetch the weather detail.

9. The **third-party API** returns the weather detail to the search page.

10. The **search page** displays the weather detail to the user.

This can also help us list out the things we need to do in the implementation.

API Design

We will need two pages for this app: A search page and a detail page. In addition, we need an endpoint for providing city suggestions based on user input.

Search Page

URL: /

Detail Page

URL: /detail/[city_id]

For example, for Seattle, the URL will be: /detail/5809844

City Suggestion Endpoint

URL: /api/city/[search_string]

For example, for searching city names with the prefix *"sea"*, the URL will be: */api/city/sea*

Task Breakdown

With the design process above, now we have a clear picture of what we should do for WeatherWise. We can break it down into the following tasks.

Preparation

1. Set up Next.js app

2. Set up OpenWeather API and acquire the API key

Search Page

3. Build the search page

4. Style the search page

City Suggestion Endpoint

5. Download the city JSON

6. Define data interface for cities

7. Implement request and response

Detail Page

8. Build the detail page

9. Define data interface for weather detail

10. Implement request to OpenWeather API

11. Style the detail page

Now with a clear picture of what to do, let's get started with coding!

Setting Up the Next.js App

As always, let's start with setting up React, Next.js, and Tailwind for this project. Refer to the entire chapter "Hello World" for initializing the app.

The process can be summarized as:

▷ **Navigate to the directory where you'd like to create the app.**

>_ cd ~/Projects/web/

▷ **Create a new Next.js web app with the name: *next-weather*.**

>_ npx create-next-app@latest next-weather

▷ **Navigate inside the app directory.**

>_ cd next-weather/

▷ **Configure TypeScript target complierOptions to *es6* in *tsconfig.json*.**

tsconfig.json (Partial)

```
{
  "compilerOptions": {
    "target": "es6",
    …
}
```

▷ **Install Tailwind CSS.**

>_ npm install -D tailwindcss postcss autoprefixer

▷ **Create Tailwind configs.**

>_ npx tailwindcss init -p

▷ **Add the paths of pages and components to *tailwind.config.js*.**

tailwind.config.js

```
/** @type {import('tailwindcss').Config} */
module.exports = {
  content: [
    "./pages/**/*.{js,ts,jsx,tsx}",
    "./components/**/*.{js,ts,jsx,tsx}",
  ],
  theme: {
    extend: {},
  },
  plugins: [],
}
```

▶ Replace the content of styles/globals.css with Tailwind directives.

styles/globals.css

```
@tailwind base;
@tailwind components;
@tailwind utilities;
```

▶ Clean up the home page, by replacing the code with the following.

pages/index.tsx

```
export default function Home() {
  return (
    <>Empty Page</>
  )
}
```

▶ Start the app

>_ npm run dev

▶ Test whether the home page is rendered correctly at http://localhost:3000. Note: the port may be different. Check the instructions in the Command Prompt.

107

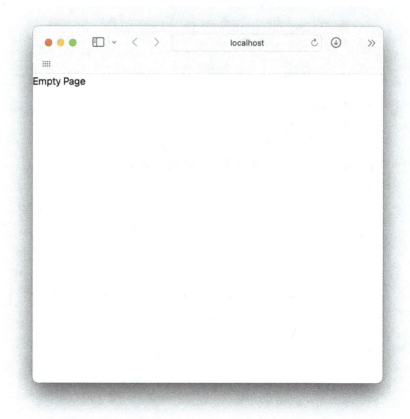

Figure 6-4: The page at http://localhost:3000/

Setting up OpenWeather API and Acquiring the API key

▷ Sign up OpenWeather and acquire an API key.

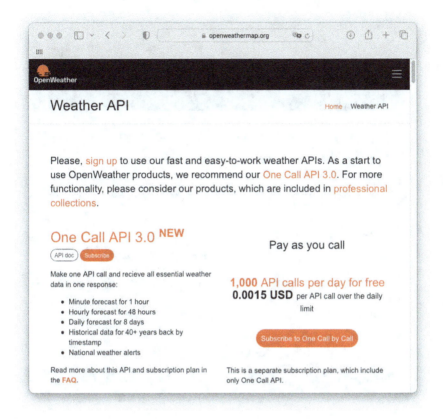

Figure 6-5: The OpenWeather API website

After you sign up for the API, create an API key. An API key is typically a long, randomly generated string of characters, like *18572971ce3b9f09fce8ce379d85113f*.

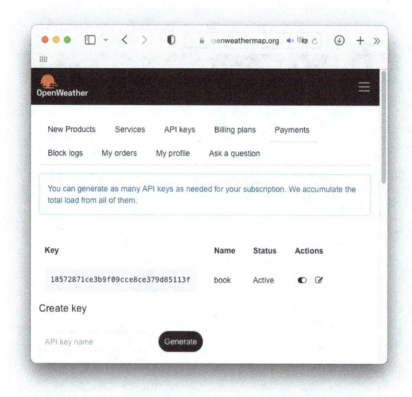

Figure 6-6: Copy the API key from your OpenWeather account

▶ **Test the Weather API, by making a cURL request with the API key.**

> curl https://api.openweathermap.org/data/2.5/weather\?lat\=47.606209\&lon\=-122.332069\&appid\=APP_ID

You may need to replace the placeholder "APP_ID" with your actual API key.

In the command line above, we use the longitude and latitude of Seattle, WA (47.606209, -122.332069).

If you receive a JSON result like the one below, it means that the API is working!

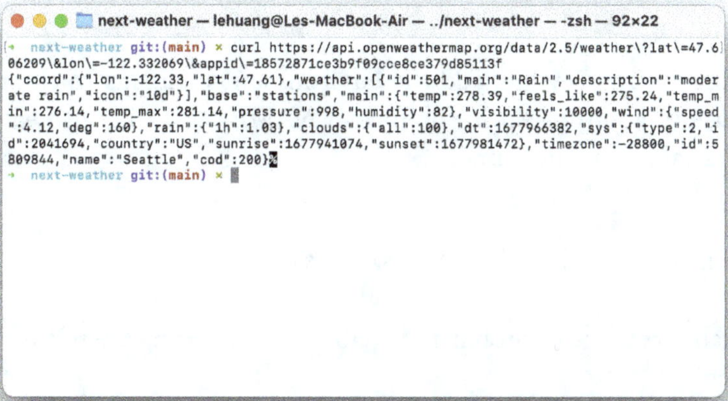

next-weather git:(main) x curl https://api.openweathermap.org/data/2.5/weather/?lat\=47.6
06209\&lon\=-122.332069\&appid\=18572871ce3b9f09cce8ce379d85113f
{"coord":{"lon":-122.33,"lat":47.61},"weather":[{"id":501,"main":"Rain","description":"moder
ate rain","icon":"10d"}],"base":"stations","main":{"temp":278.39,"feels_like":275.24,"temp_m
in":276.14,"temp_max":281.14,"pressure":998,"humidity":82},"visibility":10000,"wind":{"speed
":4.12,"deg":160},"rain":{"1h":1.03},"clouds":{"all":100},"dt":1677966382,"sys":{"type":2,"i
d":2041694,"country":"US","sunrise":1677941074,"sunset":1677981472},"timezone":-28800,"id":5
809844,"name":"Seattle","cod":200}
next-weather git:(main) x

Figure 6-7: The result from a cURL command to get weather detail for a given location

Let me explain: API keys

API keys are often used to authenticate and authorize access to web APIs, which allow software applications to interact with each other over the internet. When a user or application makes a request to an API, they include the API key as part of the request to prove their identity and permissions. The API key is checked by the API server to ensure that the requester is authorized to access the requested data or functionality.

Now, let's save the API key in the project.

▷ **Create a new file in the app directory and name it .env.**

You can either manually create this file in your code editor, or you can simply run the command line below:

```
>_ touch .env
```

Let me explain: the .env file

In Next.js, the .env file is a configuration file that allows you to set environment variables for your application. Environment variables are values that are used to configure your application's behavior in different environments, such as development, testing, and production.

Note that environment variables defined in the .env file are only available on the server side in Next.js.

▷ **Inside the .env file, add the environment variables you want to use in your project in the format NAME=VALUE, with each variable on a new line.**

<u>.env</u>

```
WEATHER_API_KEY=18572871ce3b9f09cce8ce379d85113f
```

We can access the environment variables later by using the process.env object.

For example, to access the WEATHER_API_KEY variable:

```
const apiKey = process.env.WEATHER_API_KEY;
```

Building the Search Page

We can divide the search page into two parts: the Search page and the *SearchBox* component. The *SearchBox* component will include text input and auto-suggest functionality. The Search page will contain the *SearchBox* component along with other necessary elements.

▷ **To build the search page, add a text input for the search box.**

<u>pages/index.tsx</u>

```
import SearchBox from '@/components/SearchBox'
import Head from 'next/head'

export default function Search() {
  return (
    <>
      <Head>
        <title>WeatherWise</title>
      </Head>
      <main>
        <h1>WeatherWise</h1>
        <form >
          <h2>Search for local weather</h2>
          <SearchBox />
        </form>
      </main>
    </>
  )
}
```

In the code above, we import the *Head* component from the *next/head* module. The *Head* component is used to modify the contents of the head section of the HTML document. Here, we use to set the title of the page to "*WeatherWise*" in the browser tab.

We also import the SearchBox component from the *@/components/ SearchBox* module. The @ symbol is used as a shorthand to refer to the root directory of the application.

The main element contains a heading element (*<h1>*) with the text "*WeatherWise*", a form element, and a *SearchBox* component, which we will create right after this step.

▶ **Build the SearchBox component.**

components/SearchBox.tsx

```
export default function SearchBox() {
  return (
    <>
      <input type="text" placeholder="City name" />
    </>
  )
}
```

The code above creates a component called SearchBox that renders a single text input field with a placeholder text "City name".

▶ **Check the browser, and confirm the UI looks like the following in Figure 6-8.**

Figure 6-8: The page at http://localhost:3000/

Styling the Search Page

▶ **Style the SearchBox component.**

components/SearchBox.tsx

```
export default function SearchBox() {
  return (
    <>
      <input
        className="bg-gray-200 p-2 rounded-lg w-64"
        type="text"
        placeholder="City name" />
    </>
  )
}
```

The *className* attribute sets the CSS classes for the input element. It sets the background color to gray (*bg-gray-200*), adds some padding (*p-2*), rounds the corners of the element (*rounded-lg*) and sets the width of the element to 64 pixels (*w-64*).

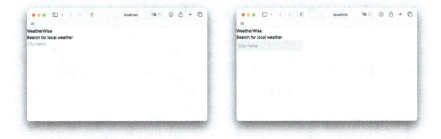

Figure 6-9: The differences between without Tailwind styles and with Tailwind styles

▷ Style the Search page.

pages/index.tsx

```
import SearchBox from '@/components/SearchBox'
import Head from 'next/head'

export default function Search() {
  return (
    <>
      <Head>
        <title>WeatherWise</title>
      </Head>
      <main className="mt-5 mx-5">
        <h1 className="text-xl font-medium mb-4">WeatherWise</h1>
        <form>
          <h2 className="text-lg  mb-4">Search for local weather</h2>
          <div className="mb-4">
            <SearchBox />
          </div>
        </form>
      </main>
    </>
  )
}
```

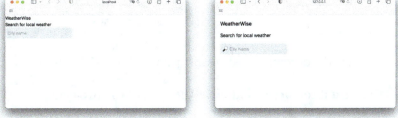

Figure 6-10: The differences between without Tailwind styles and with Tailwind styles

115

Downloading the City JSON

We need a specific city ID to query the weather detail. In the beginning, the user does not know the ID, and this is why we need to make the city suggestion endpoint to find out the city ID.

The entire dataset of cities can be found here at http://bulk.openweathermap.org/sample/city.list.json.gz.

We need to download the dataset and store it in the *lib/* directory.

▷ **Download the data set from the URL above and properly decompress. Once it is done, you should be able to get a JSON file called *city.list.json*.**

Figure 6-11: The city list JSON file is downloaded

You can see, the decompressed city.list.json is about 41.7 MB.

▷ **Create a directory called *lib* at the root of the project.**

You can manually create this directory, or run the command below in your Command Prompt at the root of the project.

```
>_ mkdir lib
```

▷ **Move the file city.list.json to *lib/*.**

116

You can manually move the file in your file system, or run the command below (if the *city.list.json* is in the *Downloads* directory, for example).

```
>_ mv ~/Downloads/city.list.json lib/
```

Defining Data Interface for City Data

City data will be exchanged between the Search page and the City Suggestion endpoint. Let's define the shape of the city data.

Let me explain: Interfaces

In Next.js, interfaces define the shape of data passed between components, pages, and the API endpoints in your application. Interfaces are a type of TypeScript feature that allows you to define the structure of an object or a function, including its properties, types, and methods.

By defining interfaces in Next.js, you can ensure that your components and pages are receiving the data they need in the correct format and that your API endpoints are returning data in the expected format.

▷ **Create a new directory called *interfaces* at the root of the project.**

You can either manually create this directory in your file system, or you can simply run the command line below, at the root of the project:

```
>_ mkdir interfaces
```

▷ **Observe the city data structure in *lib/city.list.json*.**

To design the data interface, let's take a look at how it is structured.

```
{} city.list.json ×

Users > lehuang > Downloads > {} city.list.json > ...
   1   [
   2       {
   3           "id": 833,
   4           "name": "Ḩeşār-e Sefīd",
   5           "state": "",
   6           "country": "IR",
   7           "coord": {
   8               "lon": 47.159401,
   9               "lat": 34.330502
  10           }
  11       },
  12       {
  13           "id": 2960,
  14           "name": "'Ayn Ḩalāqīm",
  15           "state": "",
  16           "country": "SY",
  17           "coord": {
  18               "lon": 36.321911,
  19               "lat": 34.940079
  20           }
  21       },
  22       {
  23           "id": 3245,
  24           "name": "Taglag",
  25           "state": "",
  26           "country": "IR",
  27           "coord": {
```

Figure 6-12: What it looks like inside the city.list.json

▷ Based on the JSON structure, create a new file called *city.ts* with the interface *CityData*.

interfaces/city.ts

```
interface CityData {
  id: number;
  name: string;
  state: string;
  country: string;
  coord: {
    lon: number;
    lat: number;
  };
}

export default CityData;
```

Implementing the City Suggestion Endpoint

▷ Create a new file called *[name].ts* under *pages/api/city/*, for the endpoint */api/city/[search_string]*.

The file name *[name].ts* uses brackets to denote the *name* parameter as a dynamic parameter that can be replaced with any value at runtime. For instance, if a user navigates to */api/city/london*, the value of *name* in the URL will be *london*.

You may wonder why we placed the aforementioned file in the directory *pages/api/*, rather than any other directory. In Next.js, any file located in the *pages/api/* folder is automatically mapped to */api/** and treated as an API endpoint, rather than a regular page.

pages/api/city/[name].ts

```
import CityData from "@/interfaces/city";
import { NextApiRequest, NextApiResponse } from "next";
import cities  from '@/lib/city.list.json';

const Cities = cities as CityData[];
const NUM_SUGGESTIONS = 5;

function searchCities(value: string):CityData[] {
  const matchingCities = Cities.filter(city =>
    city.name.toLowerCase().startsWith(value.toLowerCase())
  ).slice(0, NUM_SUGGESTIONS);

  return matchingCities;
}

export default function handler({query: {name}}: NextApiRequest, res:
NextApiResponse) {
  const cityName = Array.isArray(name) ? name.join('') : name;

  // Filter the list of cities to those whose name contains the given name
  const filteredCities = cityName? searchCities(cityName) : [];

  // Return the filtered list of cities as JSON
  return  res.json({
    cities: filteredCities
  })
}
```

First, the code imports a list of cities from the JSON file and converts it into an array of *CityData* objects.

Next, the *searchCities* function takes a string parameter and returns an array of *CityData* objects that match the string as a case-insensitive prefix. The function employs the filter method to sift through the *Cities* array based on whether the city name starts with the given value, and subsequently returns the first *NUM_SUGGESTIONS* (5) matches.

Finally, the filtered list of cities is returned as a JSON response in the Data format using the *NextApiResponse* object.

▷ **Test this endpoint.**

For instance, to request the API endpoint, navigate to http://localhost:3000/api/city/seat using a web browser.

This request should return a JSON object that contains a maximum of five cities with the prefix "*seat*".

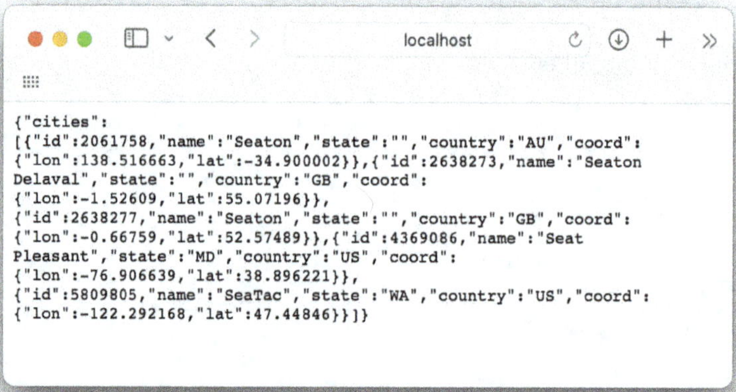

Figure 6-13: The JSON result after querying with the string "seat"

If no cities are found with the given prefix, the API endpoint should return an empty array.

For example, making a request to http://localhost:3000/api/city/abcd should result in an empty JSON array.

{"cities":[]}

Figure 6-14: The JSON result after querying with the string "abcd"

Now, we can confirm the endpoint is working as expected.

Next, we will update the logic of the *SearchBox* to retrieve city suggestions based on the user input.

▷ **Call this endpoint when the user inputs a value.**

components/SearchBox.tsx

```tsx
import React, { useEffect, useState } from "react";
import CityData from "@/interfaces/city";
import Link from "next/link";

const MIN_CITY_CHARS = 3

export default function SearchBox() {
  const [inputValue, setInputValue] = useState("");
  const [cities, setCities] = useState<CityData[]>([]);

  useEffect(() => {
    const fetchData = async () => {
      try {
        const response = await fetch(`/api/city/${inputValue}`);
        const data = await response.json();
        setCities(data.cities);

      } catch (error) {
        console.error(error);
      }
    };

    if (inputValue.length >= MIN_CITY_CHARS) {
      fetchData();
    }
  }, [inputValue]);

  return (
```

```
<>
  <input
    className="bg-gray-200 p-2 rounded-lg w-64"
    type="text"
    placeholder="City name"
    value={inputValue}
    onChange={(e) => setInputValue(e.target.value)}
  />
  {inputValue.length >= MIN_CITY_CHARS && (
    <ul>
      {cities.map((city) => (
        <li key={city.id}>
          <Link href={`/detail/${city.id}`}>
            {city.name}
            {city.state ? `, ${city.state}` : ""} ({city.country})
          </Link>
        </li>
      ))}
    </ul>
  )}
</>
  )
}
```

The component uses the *useState* hook to define two state variables,
inputValue and *cities*.

• *inputValue* is used to store the value entered in the search field.

• *cities* is used to store the list of suggested cities returned from the API.

The component uses the *useEffect* hook to fetch the suggested cities from
the API whenever the *inputValue* state variable changes. The effect is only
triggered if the length of *inputValue* is greater than or equal to the
constant *MIN_CITY_CHARS* (which is set to 3).

If the API call is successful, the list of suggested cities is stored in the
cities state variable using the *setCities* function.

Besides the original input field, the component also returns a list of
suggested cities. The list is only rendered if the length of *inputValue* is
greater than or equal to *MIN_CITY_CHARS*.

Let me explain: useState

In React, *useState* is a hook that allows functional components to have state
variables. This means that with useState, you can manage state in a functional
component without converting it to a class component.

The *useState* hook returns a pair of values: the current state value, and a function that lets you update it. The first parameter to useState is the initial state of the variable. The state variable can hold any value such as numbers, booleans, strings, objects, or arrays.

Here is an example of how to use useState:

```
import React, { useState } from 'react';

function Example() {
  const [count, setCount] = useState(0);

  return (
    <div>
      <p>You clicked {count} times</p>
      <button onClick={() => setCount(count + 1)}>Click me</button>
    </div>
  );
}
```

In this example, we define a state variable called count using the *useState* hook. The initial value of count is set to 0. We then render the current count value using the *count* variable and display a button that updates the count by calling the *setCount* function, which changes the state value.

Let me explain: useEffect

In React, *useEffect()* is a hook that allows you to perform side effects in a function component. It takes two arguments: a function that contains the side effect and an optional array of dependencies that the effect depends on.

The function passed to *useEffect()* will be executed every time the component re-renders. It can perform various side effects, such as fetching data from an API, updating the DOM, or subscribing to events.

The second argument to *useEffect()* is an optional array of dependencies. If the array is empty, the effect will only be executed once, after the initial render. If the array contains any values, the effect will be executed whenever any of those values change.

Here's an example of using *useEffect()* to fetch data from an API and update the component state:

```
import React, { useState, useEffect } from 'react';

function MyComponent() {
  const [data, setData] = useState(null);

  useEffect(() => {
    fetch('https://example.com/api/data')
      .then(response => response.json())
      .then(data => setData(data));
```

```
  }, []);

  return (
    <div>{data ? JSON.stringify(data) : 'Loading...'}</div>
  );
}
```

In this example, the component state data is initialized to null. The *useEffect()* hook is used to fetch data from an API and update the state with the received data. The empty dependency array [] ensures that the effect is only executed once, after the initial render. The component will render "Loading..." until the data is fetched and the state is updated, at which point it will display the data as a string.

The name useEffect refers to the fact that it allows you to perform "side effects" in your components, such as fetching data from an API, subscribing to events, updating the DOM, or performing other actions that don't directly relate to rendering your component.

▷ **Verify the change on the page.**

On the page http://localhost:3000/, typing "seat" will display five cities with the prefix "*seat*". It's quite cool!

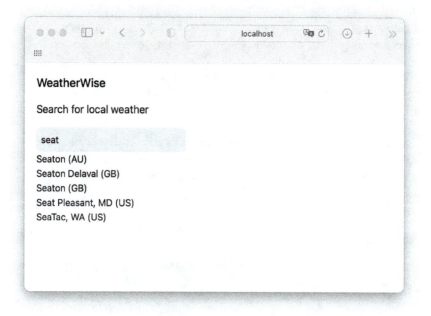

Figure 6-15: Type "seat", and get a list of cities with the prefix "seat"

Please note that the current approach is inefficient, since it sends requests on every keystroke after the user types more than two characters, even if the user is typing very quickly.

By inspecting the XHR/Fetch requests, it is easy to observe the frequent API calls.

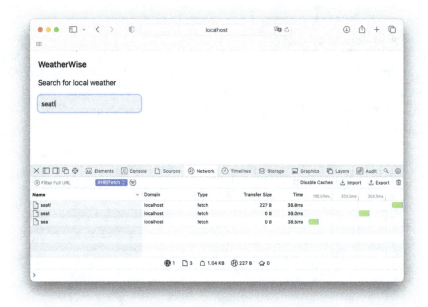

Figure 6-16: One additional key stroke triggers one new request

As seen in the above screenshot, requests are made approximately 100ms to 150ms apart, despite the user typing very quickly. The more efficient approach is to send a single request after the user pauses typing.

We can add a debounce delay to reduce the number of requests. This means that requests will only be made after a certain amount of time has passed since the user's last keystroke.

Let me explain: Debounce Delay

When you're typing something into a search box on a website, you might notice that the search results don't update immediately with every keystroke. Instead,

125

there might be a short delay before the results appear. This is done intentionally to improve the user experience and reduce unnecessary requests to the server.

A debounce function is a JavaScript function that adds a delay between subsequent calls to another function. For example, in the case of a search box, you might use a debounce function to delay the execution of a search function until the user has finished typing. This can help reduce the number of requests to the server and improve the overall performance of the website.

▶ Add debounce delay.

The typical way to set up a debounce function is: when an event comes in if there is a timer set and it does not expire yet, reset the timer and start a new timer. When the timer expires, it executes the work that needs to be done.

components/SearchBox.tsx

```tsx
import React, { useEffect, useState } from "react";
import CityData from "@/interfaces/city";
import Link from "next/link";

const MIN_CITY_CHARS = 3;

let timeoutId: ReturnType<typeof setTimeout>;
const debounce = (fn: Function, ms = 300) => {
  return function (this: any, ...args: any[]) {
    clearTimeout(timeoutId);
    timeoutId = setTimeout(() => fn.apply(this, args), ms);
  };
};

export default function SearchBox() {
  const [inputValue, setInputValue] = useState("");
  const [cities, setCities] = useState<CityData[]>([]);

  useEffect(() => {
    const fetchData = async () => {
      try {
        const response = await fetch(`/api/city/${inputValue}`);
        const data = await response.json();
        setCities(data.cities);

      } catch (error) {
        console.error(error);
      }
    };

    if (inputValue.length >= MIN_CITY_CHARS) {
      debounce(fetchData)()
    }
  }, [inputValue]);

  return (
    <>
      <input
        className="bg-gray-200 p-2 rounded-lg w-64"
```

```
        type="text"
        placeholder="City name"
        value={inputValue}
        onChange={(e) => setInputValue(e.target.value)}
      />
      {inputValue.length >= MIN_CITY_CHARS && (
        <ul>
          {cities.map((city) => (
            <li key={city.id}>
              <Link href={`/detail/${city.id}`}>
                {city.name}
                {city.state ? `, ${city.state}` : ""} ({city.country})
              </Link>
            </li>
          ))}
        </ul>
      )}
    </>
  )
}
```

▶ **Verify on the page.**

On the page http://localhost:3000/, type "*manhat*" in the input field to see a list of cities with the prefix "*manhat*".

(Fun fact, there are multiple cities named Manhattan in the world.)

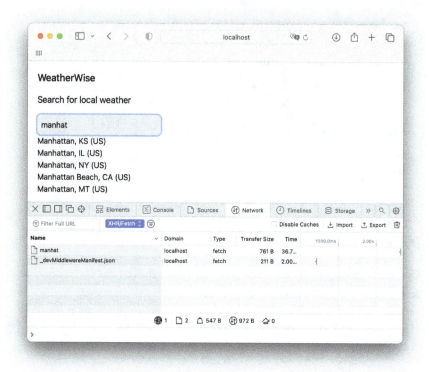

Figure 6-17: One request is only made after the user has typed "manhat" and then stops

It is also worth noting that, although the user types 6 characters, only one request is made, which is http://localhost:3000/api/city/manhat.

Building the Detail Page

The detail page displays weather information for a specific city ID and can be accessed via the URL *detail/[city_id]*.

To achieve this, we can create a page called *[city_id].tsx*.

Let me explain: [city_id].tsx

In Next.js, the file *[city_id].tsx* represents a dynamic route file with a variable number of segments in the URL path. The file name must be enclosed in square brackets [] to indicate that it is a dynamic route.

The *city_id* is a parameter name that is used in the URL path to represent the actual value that is passed in the URL. The parameter name must also be enclosed in square brackets to indicate that it is a dynamic segment.

For example, if you have a page that displays information about a city based on its ID, you can use this file to create a dynamic route that can handle URLs like /city/1, /city/2, /city/3, and so on, where the numbers at the end represent the city ID.

▷ **Create a new TSX file called [city_id].tsx under the directory /pages/detail/.**

Figure 6-18: Create a new file
called [city_id].tsx under /
pages/detail/

▷ **Create the basic page layout in [city_id].tsx.**

pages/detail/[city_id].tsx

```tsx
import Head from 'next/head'
import Link from 'next/link'

export default function () {
  return (
    <>
      <Head>
        <title>WeatherWise</title>
      </Head>
      <main>
        <div className="container">
          <Link href="/">
            &larr; Home
          </Link>
        </div>
      </main>
    </>
  )
}
```

The Link component is used to create a link to the homepage ("/").

Let me explain: the Link component

The Link component in Next.js is used for client-side navigation between pages in a Next.js application. It provides a way to create a link to a specific page in the application without requiring a full page refresh. This can help improve the performance and user experience of a web application, as it allows for faster navigation between pages.

The Link component is imported from the next/link module and is typically used in conjunction with the a element to create a clickable link. When the link is clicked, the Link component intercepts the click event and instead of requesting the new page from the server, it fetches the page from the Next.js client-side router and updates the content on the page.

Here's an example usage of the Link component:

```
import Link from 'next/link'

<Link href="/about">
  <a>About Us</a>
</Link>
```

In this example, clicking on the "About Us" link will navigate to the /about page in the application using the client-side router. The href attribute of the Link component specifies the target page for the link, while the child element specifies the text and style for the link.

▶ Verify on the page.

Navigate to http://localhost:3000/detail/5809844, where *5809844* is the ID of the city *Seattle*. This should display a basic page. Clicking the *Home* button should redirect back to the *Search* page.

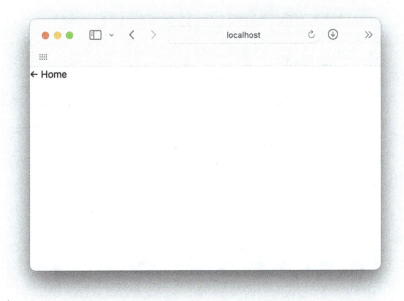

Figure 6-19: The page at http://localhost:3000/detail/5809844

Defining Data Interface for Weather Data

Similar to the city data, we now create an interface for weather data to serve as the data model.

▷ **Observe the weather data structure via the API response.**

If you recall, we did a test with the OpenWeather API. The output will tell us how the data is shaped.

Run the command below in your Command Prompt. You may need to replace the value of the app ID with your API key.

```
curl https://api.openweathermap.org/data/2.5/weather\?
lat\=47.606209\&lon\=-122.332069\&appid\=18572871ce3b9f0
9cce8ce379d85113f
```

Below is the JSON you will receive:

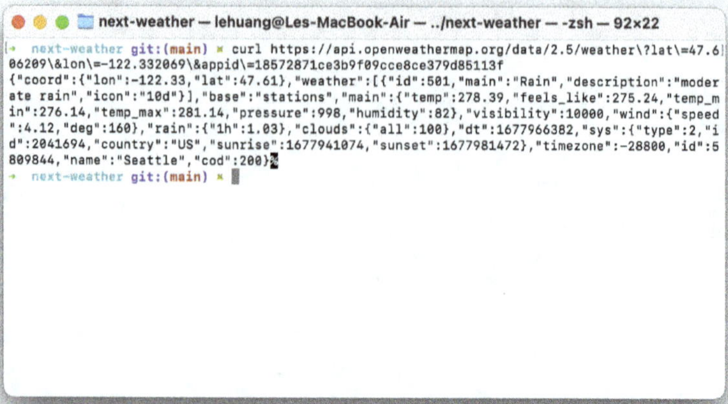

next-weather — lehuang@Les-MacBook-Air — ../next-weather — -zsh — 92×22
→ next-weather git:(main) ✗ curl https://api.openweathermap.org/data/2.5/weather\?lat\=47.606209\&lon\=-122.332069\&appid\=18572871ce3b9f09cce8ce379d85113f
{"coord":{"lon":-122.33,"lat":47.61},"weather":[{"id":501,"main":"Rain","description":"moderate rain","icon":"10d"}],"base":"stations","main":{"temp":278.39,"feels_like":275.24,"temp_min":276.14,"temp_max":281.14,"pressure":998,"humidity":82},"visibility":10000,"wind":{"speed":4.12,"deg":160},"rain":{"1h":1.03},"clouds":{"all":100},"dt":1677966382,"sys":{"type":2,"id":2041694,"country":"US","sunrise":1677941074,"sunset":1677981472},"timezone":-28800,"id":5809844,"name":"Seattle","cod":200}%
→ next-weather git:(main) ✗

Figure 6-20: The result of a cURL command to retrieve the weather detail for a given location

After formatting the JSON output, it will look like this:

```
{
  "coord": {
    "lon": -122.3321,
    "lat": 47.6062
  },
  "weather": [
    {
      "id": 800,
      "main": "Clear",
      "description": "clear sky",
      "icon": "01d"
    }
  ],
  "base": "stations",
  "main": {
    "temp": 284.76,
    "feels_like": 283.39,
    "temp_min": 281.86,
    "temp_max": 288.46,
    "pressure": 1022,
    "humidity": 54
  },
  "visibility": 10000,
  "wind": {
    "speed": 6.69,
    "deg": 320
  },
  "clouds": {
    "all": 0
  },
  "dt": 1679003480,
```

```json
  "sys": {
    "type": 2,
    "id": 2041694,
    "country": "US",
    "sunrise": 1678976441,
    "sunset": 1679019323
  },
  "timezone": -25200,
  "id": 5809844,
  "name": "Seattle",
  "cod": 200
}
```

▶ Based on the JSON example, create an interface called *Weather* in the directory of *interfaces/*.

interfaces/weather.ts

```ts
interface WeatherData {
  coord: {
    lon: number;
    lat: number;
  };
  weather: {
    id: number;
    main: string;
    description: string;
    icon: string;
  }[];
  base: string;
  main: {
    temp: number;
    feels_like: number;
    temp_min: number;
    temp_max: number;
    pressure: number;
    humidity: number;
  };
  visibility: number;
  wind: {
    speed: number;
    deg: number;
  };
  clouds: {
    all: number;
  };
  dt: number;
  sys: {
    type: number;
    id: number;
    country: string;
    sunrise: number;
    sunset: number;
  };
  timezone: number;
  id: number;
  name: string;
  cod: number;
}

export default WeatherData;
```

Implementing Request to OpenWeather API

We need to make an API call to fetch weather data from an external source on the server side.

To achieve this, we will implement the API call inside the *getServerSideProps()* function.

▷ Call the Weather API to get the weather data

pages/detail/[city_id].tsx

```
import CityData from '@/interfaces/city';
import WeatherData from '@/interfaces/weather';
import cities from "@/lib/city.list.json"
import { GetServerSidePropsContext } from 'next';
import Head from 'next/head'
import Link from 'next/link'

let Cities = cities as CityData[]

export async function getServerSideProps(context: GetServerSidePropsContext)
{

  const { city_id } = context.query

  // Find the city why city Id
  const city = Cities.find((city) => city.id.toString() == city_id);

  if (!city) {
    throw new Error("City not found");
  }

  let url = `https://api.openweathermap.org/data/2.5/weather?lat=$
{city.coord.lat}&lon=${city.coord.lon}&appid=${process.env.WEATHER_API_KEY}
&exclude=minutely&units=metric`

  // Fetch the weather data
  const res = await fetch(url);

  const weatherData: WeatherData = await res.json();

  if (!weatherData) {
    throw new Error("Weather data not found");
  }

  return {
    props: {
      city: city,
      weather: weatherData
    }
  };
}

type Props = {
  city: CityData
  weather: WeatherData
```

134

```
}
export default function ({ city, weather }: Props) {
  return (
    <>
      <Head>
        <title>WeatherWise</title>
      </Head>
      <main>
        <div className="container">
          <Link href="/">
            &larr; Home
          </Link>
          <h1>{city.name} ({city.country})</h1>
          <h2>
            {weather.main.temp_max.toFixed(0)}&deg;C
{weather.main.temp_min.toFixed(0)}&deg;C
          </h2>
          <div>{weather.weather[0].description}</div>
        </div>
      </main>
    </>
  )
}
```

▶ **Verify on the page.**

To view the weather details for Seattle, navigate to the URL http://
localhost:3000/detail/5809844.

Figure 6-21: The page at http://localhost:3000/detail/5809844

135

To test the end-to-end user experience, navigate to the Search page at http://localhost:3000/ and search for a city, such as "*Seattle*". Then, click on the city name to be redirected to the detail page as shown above.

Displaying An Image

We would like to include an image provided by the OpenWeather API to enhance the visual representation of the weather information. The image is a visual display that represents the weather conditions.

Since this image is from an external website, we need to ensure that we properly implement it in our Next.js application.

Let's proceed with the necessary steps to properly display the image.

▷ **Add the Image component.**

pages/detail/[city_id].tsx

```
import CityData from '@/interfaces/city';
import WeatherData from '@/interfaces/weather';
import cities from "@/lib/city.list.json"
import { GetServerSidePropsContext } from 'next';
import Head from 'next/head';
import Link from 'next/link';
import Image from 'next/image';

let Cities = cities as CityData[]

export async function getServerSideProps(context: GetServerSidePropsContext)
{

  const { city_id } = context.query

  // Find the city why city Id
  const city = Cities.find((city) => city.id.toString() == city_id);

  if (!city) {
    throw new Error("City not found");
  }

  let url = `https://api.openweathermap.org/data/2.5/weather?lat=$
{city.coord.lat}&lon=${city.coord.lon}&appid=${process.env.WEATHER_API_KEY}
&exclude=minutely&units=metric`

  // Fetch the weather data
  const res = await fetch(url);

  const weatherData: WeatherData = await res.json();

  if (!weatherData) {
    throw new Error("Weather data not found");
  }
}
```

```
  return {
    props: {
      city: city,
      weather: weatherData
    }
  };
}

type Props = {
  city: CityData
  weather: WeatherData
}

export default function ({ city, weather }: Props) {
  const iconUrl = `https://openweathermap.org/img/wn/$
{weather.weather[0].icon}@2x.png`
  return (
    <>
      <Head>
        <title>WeatherWise</title>
      </Head>
      <main>
        <div>
          <Link href="/">
            &larr; Home
          </Link>
          <h1>{city.name} ({city.country})</h1>
          <h2>
            {weather.main.temp_max.toFixed(0)}&deg;C
{weather.main.temp_min.toFixed(0)}&deg;C
          </h2>
          <div>{weather.weather[0].description}</div>
          <Image src={iconUrl} width={50} height={50} alt="Weather Icon" />
        </div>
      </main>
    </>
  )
}
```

Let me explain: the Image Component

In Next.js, the Image component is an optimized tool for handling images in an
application. It offers automatic optimization of images with features such as lazy
loading and image resizing, which don't require any additional configurations.

Here's an example:

```
import Image from 'next/image'

function MyImage() {
  return (
    <Image
      src="/images/my-image.jpg"
      alt="My image"
      width={500}
      height={500}
    />
  )
}
```

137

The example above utilizes the Image component to exhibit an image file. The src attribute defines the path to the image file, while the alt attribute is used to describe the image for accessibility purposes. The width and height attributes specify the image's dimensions, which are necessary for Next.js to optimize the image for performance.

By default, the Image component uses the img HTML tag to display the image, but it can also use the picture tag for more complex image needs. Additionally, the Image component can handle responsive images by specifying different sizes of the image for various device sizes.

▷ **Verify on the page.**

After following the previous step, you may notice that the image is not displayed on the page http://localhost:3000/detail/5809844, and an error is displayed instead:

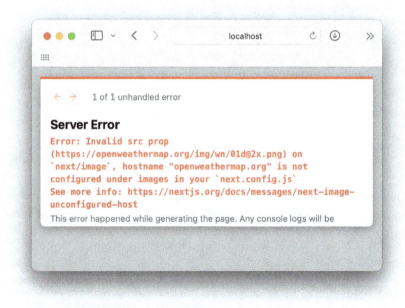

Figure 6-22: The error message for not whitelisting an external image

Next.js, as a security precaution, requires explicit allowlisting of images from external domains such as openweathermap.org, in order to ensure secure handling of the image.

This is something that we may not consider when building something with pure HTML.

▷ **Whitelist the hostname of the image in next.config.js**

<u>next.config.js</u>

```
/** @type {import('next').NextConfig} */
const nextConfig = {
  reactStrictMode: true,
  images: {
    domains: ['openweathermap.org'],
  },
}

module.exports = nextConfig
```

▷ **Make sure to restart the service after this change in next.config.js.**

To restart the service, terminate the current session by pressing Cmd + C in the Command Prompt. Next, run the following command to start the service again:

```
>_ npm run dev
```

▷ **Verify on the page.**

If the whitelisting process is successful, you will be able to view the image that displays the current weather on the page http:// localhost:3000/detail/5809844.

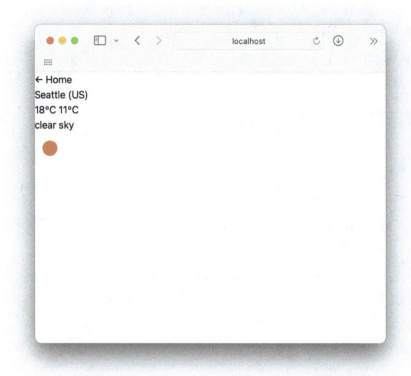

Figure 6-23: The page at http://localhost:3000/detail/5809844, with no error

Please note that the image you see may look different from the one shown above depending on the current weather conditions.

Styling the Detail page

While the UI is functional, it may not look visually appealing. To enhance the UI, we can use Tailwind CSS.

▷ **Update the UI with HTML changes and Tailwind Styles.**

<u>pages/detail/[city_id].tsx (Partial)</u>

```
export default function ({ city, weather }: Props) {
  const iconUrl = `https://openweathermap.org/img/wn/$
{weather.weather[0].icon}@2x.png`
  return (
```

140

```
<>
  <Head>
    <title>WeatherWise</title>
  </Head>
  <main className="mt-5 mx-5">
    <h1 className="text-xl font-medium mb-4">WeatherWise</h1>
    <Link href="/" className="text-sm">
      &larr; Home
    </Link>
    <div className="py-5">
      <div className="bg-blue-500 rounded p-4">
        <div className="grid grid-cols-2">
          <div>
            <h2 className="text-2xl mb-4 text-white">{city.name}
({city.country})</h2>
            <span className="font-medium text-lg text-white">
              {weather.main.temp_max.toFixed(0)}&deg;C
            </span>
             
            <span className="text-gray-300 text-sm">
              {weather.main.temp_min.toFixed(0)}&deg;C
            </span>
          </div>
          <div className="justify-self-end">
            <Image src={iconUrl} width={50} height={50} alt="Weather
Icon" />
            <div className="text-white text-sm">
              {weather.weather[0].description}
            </div>
          </div>
        </div>
      </div>
    </div>
  </main>
</>
  )
}
```

▷ **Verify on the UI.**

To view the updated UI, navigate to the URL http://localhost:3000/detail/5809844.

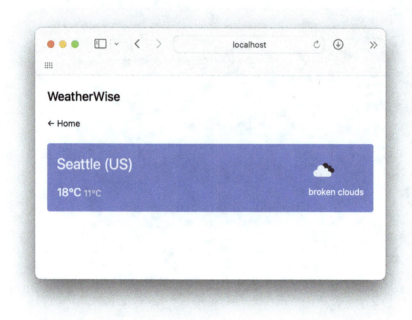

Figure 6-24: The page at http://localhost:3000/detail/5809844 has been updated with Tailwind styles.

You can also go back to http://localhost:3000/, to test the end-to-end user experience. By this point, we have just finished building a functional and visually appealing weather app!

Code Example

You can find the complete code for this weather app at: https://github.com/higracehuang/next-weather.

If you ever feel confused while following the tutorials, you can refer to this link for guidance.

Conclusion

Congratulations on completing another project using the Dynamic Trio of web development tools.

In this chapter, you created a dynamic and interactive website that displays content based on user input.

We covered the following key concepts:

Setting up a third-party API

After signing up for the OpenWeather API, we acquired an API key and tested the API using the cURL command.

In Next.js, API keys are stored in the *.env* file.

Defining interfaces

In this application, the exchanged data consists of city data and weather data.

To maintain the integrity of the data, we utilized the interface concept in TypeScript and defined interfaces for both city data and weather data.

Making external requests

Since this application relies on data from OpenWeather, we implemented making external service requests to the OpenWeather API within the *getServerProps()* function.

Displaying images

To display an image, we used the *Image* component in Next.js to leverage features that a pure *<img>* tag doesn't provide.

For security reasons, if the image is sourced from an external domain, additional whitelisting within the app is required.

Styling pages with Tailwind

Finally, we used various styles from Tailwind to clean up the page and make the page visually appealing.

Although we have built several apps together, we cannot consider them complete until we deploy them to production.

Let's focus on deploying the app in the next chapter to ensure it is fully functional and accessible to users

CHAPTER 7: DEPLOYING TO PRODUCTION

Deploying your application to production is the final step in bringing your hard work to the world. It's a critical process that requires careful planning and attention to detail.

In this chapter, we'll guide you through the steps to ensure a successful deployment to production.

Goals of this Chapter

In this chapter, we will cover the following topics:

• Deploying to Production

• Domain setup

• Monitoring

Deploying to Production

Cloud Provider Options

Before deploying a Next.js app, it's important to choose a cloud provider that offers specific integrations and optimizations for this type of application.

Some popular options include AWS, Google Cloud Platform, Microsoft Azure, Heroku, and Vercel.

The easiest and most streamlined way to deploy a Next.js app is by using Vercel, which was created by the same company that developed the Next.js framework and is specifically designed for its deployment and management.

Let me explain: why Vercel is the easiest deployment option

- **Zero-config deployment**: Vercel provides zero-config deployment, meaning it can automatically detect and configure your Next.js app's environment. This means you don't need to worry about configuring your app for deployment - Vercel takes care of it for you.

- **Built-in serverless functions**: Vercel provides built-in support for serverless functions, which are a key feature of Next.js. This means you can easily deploy your app and its serverless functions to the same platform.

- **Global CDN**: Vercel has a global content delivery network (CDN) that ensures your app loads quickly for users around the world. This is especially important for Next.js apps, which can be server-rendered and require fast response times.

- **Integration with Git**: Vercel integrates with Git, making it easy to deploy your app directly from your code repository. This means you can deploy changes to your app automatically as soon as you push them to your repository.

- **Easy collaboration**: Vercel makes it easy to collaborate with other developers on your Next.js app. You can invite team members to your Vercel project, and they can deploy changes to the app directly from their local development environment.

- **Low initial cost**: At the time of writing (2023), Vercel offers free access for personal and non-commercial projects, making it an affordable option for individuals looking to gain hands-on experience with the technology.

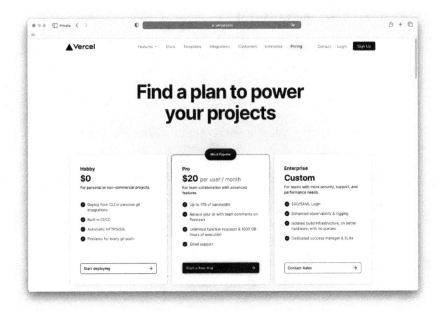

Figure 7-1: The pricing page for Vercel

In this book, we will focus on deploying to Vercel as our cloud provider. However, depending on your specific needs or your company's requirements, it may be worth exploring other cloud providers as well.

There are two methods for deploying to Vercel:

- Through Vercel CLI

- Via a Git Repository.

Deployment through Vercel CLI

Here are the steps for deploying your website via Vercel CLI.

▷ **Create a Vercel account at https://vercel.com.**

▷ **Install the Vercel CLI.**

To install the CLI, open the terminal and run the following command:

```
>_ npm install -g vercel
```

▷ **Connect your app to Vercel.**

In your Command Prompt, navigate to your Next.js app directory and run the following command:

>_ `vercel login`

The Command Prompt will display prompts with login options.

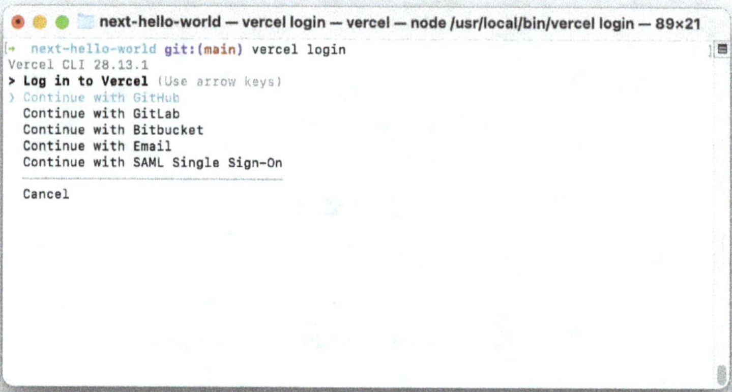

Figure 7-2: The prompts after typing *vercel login*

▷ **Deploy your app.**

Run the following command in the app directory:

>_ `vercel deploy`

Wait until the deployment to complete. This process may take a few minutes.

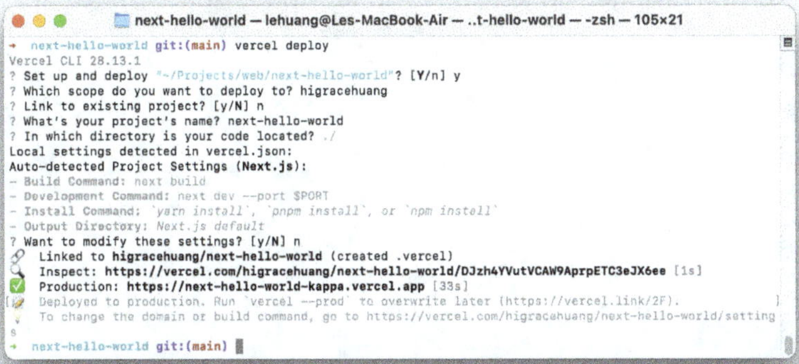

Figure 7-3: The prompts after typing *vercel deploy*

▷ **Verify the website is running.**

Once it is complete, it will generate a URL for your website.

In this example, the deployed URL is https://next-hello-world-kappa.vercel.app/. Please note that your URL may be different, but it should have a subdomain of *vercel.app*. You can go to the URL and verify it is running.

Figure 7-4: The page is hosted on the vercel domain, after deployment

Congratulations! Your website is currently serving the public.

You should also see a new app showing up on your Vercel dashboard at https://vercel.com/dashboard.

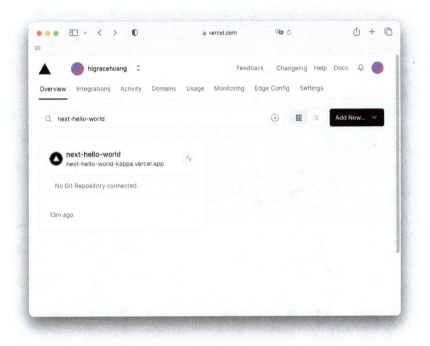

Figure 7-5: The Vercel dashboard for the deployed app

You may have noticed the text "No Git Repository connected" in the screenshot above. This is because the deployment was directly initiated from the CLI and was not connected to any repository.

Another way to deploy to Vercel is through a Git repository.

Deployment via a Git Repository

Before using this deployment method, you must have an account with a Git repository provider, such as GitHub, GitLab, or Bitbucket.

Here are the steps for deploying your website via a Git Repository. I will use Github as an example.

▷ **Create a Vercel account at <u>https://vercel.com</u>.**

▷ **Commit your app to the GitHub repository.**

▷ **On the Vercel dashboard, connect your GitHub account.**

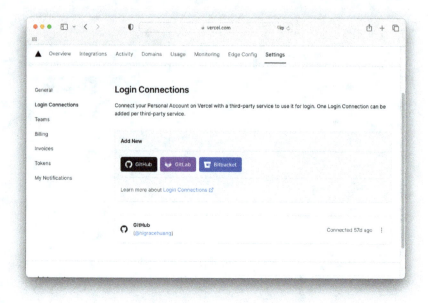

Figure 7-6: Options to connect your code repositories

▷ **Import and deploy the app.**

On the Vercel dashboard, choose *"Add New Project"*, *"Import"* the project you prefer, and then hit *Deploy*.

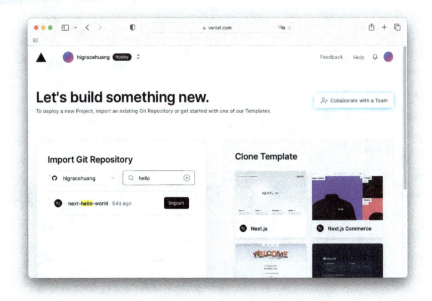

Figure 7-7: Import your Git repository

At this point, the deployment process has been initiated!

▷ **Once the deployment is complete, verify the website is running.**

In this example, a new Vercel domain has been generated: <u>https://next-hello-world-xi.vercel.app/</u>. To verify that the correct page is displayed, simply open the URL in a web browser and confirm that the page loads as expected.

The main advantage of deploying via a Git repository is that any changes pushed to the remote repository are immediately deployed to the website.

Setting up Domain

At this point, your application is deployed and running smoothly on Vercel under the *.vercel.app* domain.

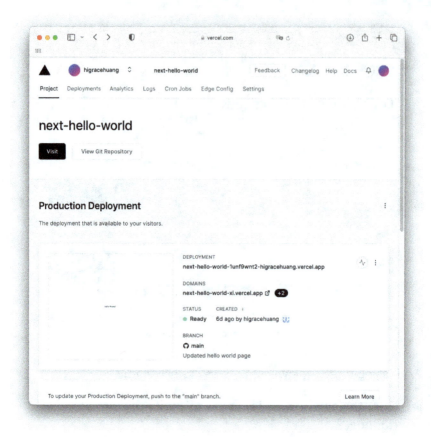

Figure 7-8: The app belongs to a subdomain of the vercel.app domain

If you wish to have your custom domain host the website you have built on Vercel, you can easily set it up. Let's take a look at how it's done.

▷ **Register a domain name based on your preference.**

To obtain a domain name for your website, you can visit a domain registrar such as GoDaddy, Namecheap, or Google Domains. Once there, you can search for available domain names and purchase the one you prefer.

In this example, we will use the domain name "*ilovedata.io*" which I currently own at the registrar Namecheap.

▷ **On the Vercel dashboard, type in the new domain.**

Go to the *Project Settings* and select the *Domains* section. Then, enter your domain name (e.g. ilovedata.io) in the input field provided (Figure 7-9).

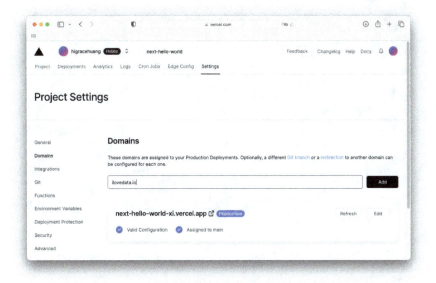

Figure 7-9: Add the new domain

▷ **Add the domain.**

When you add your domain, you will typically be asked to choose between three options (Figure 7-10): no redirection, redirect to www, or redirect to non-www.

It is recommended to choose the first option, which allows your website to work on both the non-www and www versions of your domain.

When a user enters the non-www version of your domain (e.g. ilovedata.io), they will be automatically redirected to the www version (e.g. www.ilovedata.io).

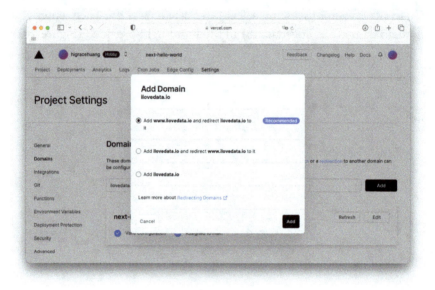

Figure 7-10: Choose the option, which allows your website to work on both the non-www and www versions of your domain

Once the domains are added, both domains would show Invalid Configuration, and you need to configure them on the dashboard of your registrar (for example, Namecheap in this case).

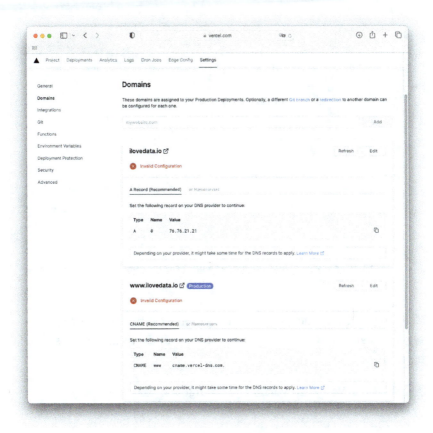

Figure 7-11: Expected warning messages after the domain is added

The warning messages on the Vercel dashboard will provide you with change suggestions that you will need to make on your registrar's website, including updating your A record and CNAME record.

▷ **Update the A record and CNAME record accordingly on your registrar.**

As an example, if you are using Namecheap as your domain registrar, below (Figure 7-12) is what it may look like after you have updated both the A record and the CNAME record.

Figure 7-12: Update both CNAME Record and A Record on the domain registrar, for example,
Namecheap in the example

Keep in mind that the user interface may look different for other
registrars such as GoDaddy or Google Domains, but the process should
be similar.

▷ **Wait for Vercel to verify the changes.**

Once you have completed the above step correctly, wait for some time
and check the Vercel dashboard.

If everything is configured correctly, you will see blue checkmarks next
to your domain configurations (Figure 7-13). This means that the
configuration and linking were successful and your domain will soon be
linked to your application.

However, it's important to note that DNS propagation can take 24-48
hours in general, so it may take some time for the domain to start
working for all users. In some cases, it may happen faster - for example,
in my case, it only took about 5 minutes.

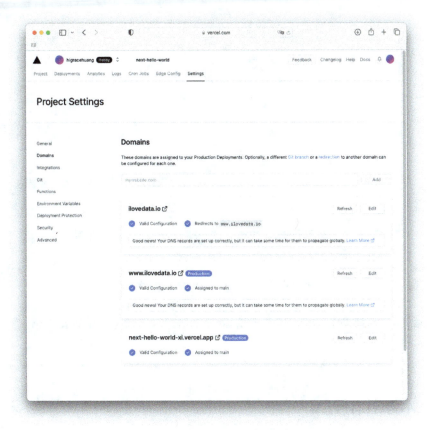

Figure 7-13: The new domain is applied successfully

▷ **Verify the domain in the browser.**

Go to your newly linked domain. In this example, *https://www.ilovedata.io/*, and check if it shows the content of your Vercel app, which is *https://next-hello-world-xi.vercel.app/*.

Figure 7-14: The page shown at the new domain

Great work! Your domain is now set up and linked to your Vercel app successfully.

Monitoring

Once your website is deployed to production and your domain is set up, it's important to monitor its health and performance to ensure that it's running smoothly and providing the best possible user experience.

Monitoring your website can help you identify and address any issues before they become significant problems, and can also provide valuable insights into how your users are interacting with your site.

In this section, we will explore some tools you can use to keep track of your website's performance. If you are an individual website owner, these tools will be very helpful.

Vercel Analytics

Vercel provides basic analytics and logs to monitor your site.

These functionalities come for free if you deploy using Vercel. It only requires you to enable the functionality on the Vercel dashboard.

Some of the benefits of using Vercel's analytics and logs include:

Real-time monitoring of website performance: With Vercel analytics, you can monitor the performance of your website in real time, including metrics like *page load time, time to interactive,* and more. This can help you identify any performance issues and optimize your website for faster load times.

Debugging with stack traces and error messages: Vercel logs provide detailed information about any errors that occur on your website, including stack traces and error messages. (See Figure 7-15 for an example of Vercel logs)

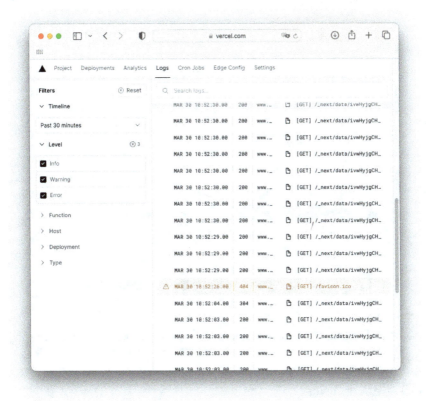

Figure 7-15: The server log at Vercel dashboard

Understanding user behavior: By using Vercel analytics, you can gain insights into how your users are interacting with your website, including which pages are most popular, where users are coming from, and more.

Optimizing website content: Vercel analytics can help you identify which pages and content are performing best, and optimize your website accordingly. (See Figure 7-16 for an example of Vercel analytics)

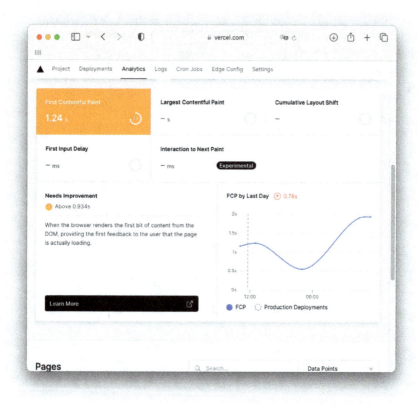

Figure 7-16: Based on the Vercel analytics, you can optimize your website based on the data

Google Analytics

Google Analytics is another key tool for website owners. It is a free web analytics service offered by Google that tracks and reports website traffic.

It provides website owners with insights into how users interact with their website, including metrics such as page views, bounce rate, session duration, and more.

With Google Analytics, website owners can gain a deeper understanding of their audience, optimize their website's performance, and make data-driven decisions about their online marketing efforts.

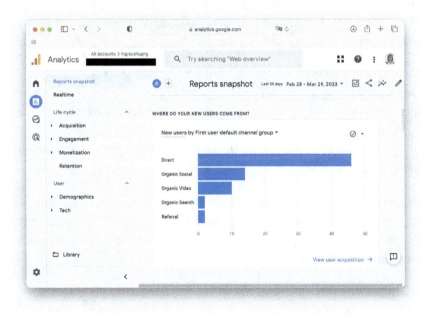

Figure 7-17: Google Analytics shows traffic sources to your website

At the time of writing this book, Google Analytics provides more comprehensive analytics on traffic, user bases, and site performance.

To use Google Analytics, create an account and set up a new property for your website. This will provide you with a tracking ID and a JavaScript code snippet to add to your website.

CONCLUSION

Congratulations on completing this book on building web applications with Dynamic Trio - React, Next.js, and Tailwind! I hope that you have found this book informative, practical, and enjoyable to read.

Through this book, you have learned about the fundamentals of React, Next.js, and Tailwind, and how these frameworks can be used to create scalable and responsive web applications. We have covered the basics of each framework, including how to set up a development environment, create components, and manage the state. Additionally, we have explored more advanced topics, such as server-side rendering, static site generation, and styling with Tailwind.

Moreover, we have provided you with project examples that demonstrate how to use these frameworks in real-world scenarios. These projects include a simple Hello World application, a blog, and a weather application. By following these examples, you should have a good understanding of how to structure and build complex web applications using React, Next.js, and Tailwind.

However, this book is just the beginning of your journey in building web applications. There are many more resources available that can help you deepen your knowledge and expertise in these frameworks. Here are a few resources that we recommend:

- **Official documentation**: The official documentation for React, Next.js, and Tailwind is an excellent resource for learning more about these frameworks. It provides detailed information on each feature, API, and configuration option.

- **Online communities**: There are many online communities where developers can share their experiences and learn from one another. Examples include Reddit's React, Next.js, and Tailwind subreddits, Twitter, and Stack Overflow.

- **YouTube**: YouTube is an excellent resource for learning about React, Next.js, and Tailwind. There are many channels dedicated to teaching these frameworks and watching video tutorials can be a great way to supplement your learning. I sometimes share tips about building web applications on my channel https://www.youtube.com/@TipsByGraceHuang.

I hope that this book has helped you to develop your skills in building web applications with React, Next.js, and Tailwind.

Whether it's a personal project or a commercial application, I can't wait to see what you will build!

ABOUT AUTHOR

Grace Huang was a software engineer at several big tech companies, including Amazon, and Bloomberg. Grace co-founded a hardware / AI company, Roxy. The product line was later acquired and the team joined Twitter. Since leaving Twitter, Grace has been focusing on writing and teaching.

Other technical books that Grace wrote:

- Build macOS Apps With SwiftUI: A Practical Learning Guide (https://amzn.to/40PUpzu)

- Nail A Coding Interview: Six-Step Mental Framework (https://amzn.to/3nZ16kp)

- Code Reviews In Tech: The Missing Guide (https://gracehuang.gumroad.com/l/codereviews)

- A Practical Guide to Writing a Software Technical Design Document (https://gracehuang.gumroad.com/l/mqmUt)

You can reach Grace at @imgracehuang on Twitter.

www.ingramcontent.com/pod-product-compliance
Lightning Source LLC
LaVergne TN
LVHW051735050326
832903LV00023B/923